Film Remakes as Ritual and Disguise

Film Remakes as Ritual and Disguise

From Carmen to Ripley

Anat Zanger

AMSTERDAM UNIVERSITY PRESS

Front cover illustration: *Carmen* (1983), directed by Carlos Saura
© Emiliano Piedro / Television Española

Back cover illustration: *Carmen* (1984), directed by Francesco Rosi, with Julia Migenes-Johnson as Carmen. Picture from ASAP collections

ISBN-13   978 90 5356 784 5 (paperback)
ISBN-10   90 5356 784 4 (paperback)

ISBN-13   978 90 5356 785 2 (hardcover)
ISBN-10   90 5356 785 2 (hardcover)

NUR   674

© Amsterdam University Press, Amsterdam 2006

Table of Contents

Part Two   Second Variation: Joan

Conclusion

Acknowledgments

I would like to express my gratitude to the French Government (1999-2000), Prof. Nilly Cohen, former Rector of Tel Aviv University, Prof. Nurith Kenaan-Kedar, former Dean of the Faculty of the Arts and the Tel Aviv University Research Authority for research grants (2000-2001) that have made this book possible. My research was carried out in archives and libraries of the British Film Institute and the Huntley Archives (London), *La Cinémathèque Français*, BiFi – *Bibliothèque du film* and *La Bibliothèque-Musée de l'Opéra National de France* (Paris), *Centre National de la cinématographie, Archives du Film*, Bois d'Arcy, *Centre Jeanne d'Arc* (Orléans), France, *Filmmuseum* (Amsterdam) and The Film Archives at Overveen (Netherlands), the UCLA Archives (Los Angeles), the MOMA Archives (New York), The Library of Congress (Washington, DC) and the Israeli Cinematheque (Jerusalem) and the Anda Zimand Film Archive Film & Television Department at Tel Aviv University. I would like to thank all these archives and libraries for the use of their facilities.

My first meeting with the subject of repetition in films came about during research for my Ph.D. dissertation at the School of Cultural Studies at Tel Aviv University. My doctoral work was supervised by Prof. Brian McHale (formerly of Tel Aviv University, now of Ohio State University, Columbus) to whom I owe a deep debt of gratitude for his illuminating comments and for his consistent interest and encouragement. I would also like to thank Prof. Edward Turk, Prof. Henry Jenkins and Prof. Peter Donaldson of the Department of Media Studies at MIT, where I continued my research. Many thanks are also due to Prof. Daniel Dayan, Prof. Linda Dittmar and Prof. Vivian Sobchack, of CNRS (France), UCLA, and University of Massachusetts (Boston), respectively, for their comments and encouragement in the earliest phases of the project.

Partial and early versions of the second chapter of the book on the multiple versions of *Carmen* were presented at international conferences and lectures at the MIT Department of Media Studies (1996), the Second International Conference of the Film and Television Department of Tel Aviv University (1998), the Popular Music and the Media Conference at the University of Sheffield, UK (2000), and the University of Newcastle upon Tyne, UK (2002). The findings were published in *Assaph Kolnoa: Studies in Cinema & Television* (2): 55-71 (2001). A partial version of Chapter 7 was presented at the SCS Conference at La Jolla, California (1998) and published by the Porter Institute of Tel Aviv University (2000). Chapter 4 is based on an article entitled "Desire Ltd: On Romanies, Women, and Other Smugglers in *Carmen*" published in *Framework*'s special issue on cinematic images of Romanies. Guest editor Dina Iordanova (44) 2: 81-94, Fall, 2003. I wish to thank the respective publishers and editors for publishing my essays and for allowing me to reprint them in this book, in each case in a somewhat altered or revised form.

I owe special thanks to Prof. Freddie Rokem, Dean of the Faculty of the Arts and to my colleagues and friends at the Film and Television Department at Tel Aviv University, especially Prof. Mihal R. Friedman, Prof. Nurith Gertz, Prof. Yehouda (Judd) Ne'eman, Dr. Dubi Rubenstein and Orna Erez who supported and encouraged me during different phases of this project.

I would like to express my deepest gratitude to Chaya Amir and Ruth Ruzga for copy-editing this manuscript with great care and insightfulness. Finally, I would like to express my appreciation to my mother, Hedva (Maimon) Zanger, and my late father, Kopel Zanger, for their support and encouragement, and to my daughter Tal who, from the time she was two years old, shared with me all of my travels, endless sessions in archives and libraries, and who sat through many of the video versions; she was, more recently, responsible for the graphic side of the manuscript.

Anat Zanger
Tel Aviv, December 2005

Introduction

> The traditional history of culture takes into consideration for each chrono-
> logical section only "new" texts, texts created by the given age. But in the
> real existence of culture, texts transmitted by the given cultural tradition or
> introduced from outside always function side by side with new texts.
> (Juri Lotman, 1978)

Cinema as a social institution knows what Scheherazade seems to have known all along: to narrate is to triumph over death. Hence, in an ongoing ceremony that occurs in the darkness of the movie theater (and lasts, ultimately, more than 1001 nights), society constantly delivers its encoded messages. The constant re-petition of the same tale keeps it alive in social memory, continually transmit-ting its meaning and relevance. It is in this context that I suggest that the pre-sence of repetitive chains of remakes can be identified as "hidden streams" (Bazin's term, 1955) in the imaginary archive of the cinema.

The tendency of cinema to produce a "remake" that retells a previously suc-cessful story has to be accounted for in the light of the medium's unique capa-city for reproduction. Given the fact that recorded versions already exist, what is the purpose of re-addressing and re-articulating the same story time and again? The aim of this book is to trace the cultural and aesthetic *instrumentalities* of the chains of remakes and to locate the remake as part of the cinematic insti-tution that has shaped and reshaped collective imagination through the sites of its pleasures, fears and traumas.

The relationship between original and version encapsulates the dialectic of repetition, the dialectic between old and new, before and after, desire and fulfill-ment. Using the tales of *Psycho*, *Carmen* and *Joan of Arc* as its navigators, *Film Remakes as Ritual and Disguise* explores the phenomenon of *multi-versions* as one that illuminates the preferences and politics of the cinematic apparatus through its choices of repetition and differentiation.

One of the most popular series that the cinema has produced stems from Alfred Hitchcock's film PSYCHO (1960). Cinema (and culture) embraced PSYCHO and endowed it with a "cult" status, complete with quotations, allusions, ho-mages, and direct and indirect transformations. Three sequels have so far been made – by Richard Franklin (1983), Anthony Perkins (1986), and Mick Garris (1990). Homage was paid to PSYCHO with pastiches like Tobe Hooper's TEXAS CHAINSAW MASSACRE (1974), John Carpenter's HALLOWEEN (1974) and Brian de

Palma's DRESSED TO KILL (1980). To that one might add Douglas Gordon's video installation 24 Hour Psycho (1993) and the installation at the Hitchcock exhibition at the Pompidou, Paris (2001). But it is Gus Van Sant's 1998 remake and declared homage to PSYCHO that overtly discusses the question of cinematic repetitions. I will be using PSYCHO to trace the dynamics of repetitions within the framework of the horror genre which operates in and vis-à-vis mainstream cinematic conventions.

Over fifty cinematic versions of the Carmen story and almost forty of the Joan of Arc story have been produced to date. There are fewer remakes of (or sequels to) such works as Anna Karenina, The Three Musketeers, The Decameron, Don Quixote, Faust, the Cleopatra story or any of Shakespeare's plays.[1] This previously unnoticed "statistic" is clearly charged with meaning: both the Carmen and the Joan stories deal with exceptional female heroines who challenge social conventions and die as a result. This would suggest that a social narrative, as defined by Jameson, underlies the empirical data of each of these numerous retellings. I interpret the exceptional number of these repetitions as evidence of Western society's inability to come to terms with women who do not conform. By ritualistically exorcising them over and over again, the cinema is delineating areas of social denial.

Apart from being among the most frequently filmed stories in cinema history, the stories of Carmen and Joan have been produced by some of cinema's most distinguished directors: Georges Méliès, Cecil B. DeMille, Charlie Chaplin, Jacques Feyder, Raoul Walsh, Carl Dreyer, Ernst Lubitsch, Charles Vidor, Otto Preminger, Roberto Rossellini, Robert Bresson, Francesco Rosi, Peter Brook, Jean-Luc Godard and Luc Besson. Given the vast number of known versions in both chains, I do not deal with them all. My choice of films was guided by the accessibility of materials on the one hand and, on the other, by the desire to provide a chronological and generic sampling of each corpus that would allow the examination of significant aesthetic and socio-cultural instances of repetition.

Cinematic versions of the Carmen and Joan stories have appeared repeatedly, from the inception of cinema to the present day, and so constitute sequential chains which enable us to investigate specific shifts in the cinematic medium, as well as in general cultural norms. As a theoretical umbrella, I will use the "institutional approach," based primarily on work by Pierre Bourdieu (1979), Itamar Even-Zohar (1990), Noël Carroll (1996) and Steve (Stephen) Neale (1980, 1990). Despite their differences, all four understand "institution" as a system that maintains a specific medium as a socio-cultural activity (e.g., literature, painting or cinema). Revolving around institutional, intertextual and feminist issues, the present book elaborates upon – and at times challenges – contemporary studies on related subjects. The weaving together of these theories produces a "symptomatic" reading of the phenomenon of the remake as a response to changing norms in cinema and provides an understanding of their function as a socio-cultural agent within the cinematic market. By presenting three test cases that run the gamut of cinematic history, I hope to illuminate the relations between these obstinate repetitions and the cinema as part of the "cultural field of production."

In terms of cinema as a social and cultural memory, the book asks two sets of questions. The first: What are the possible relations among cultural, literary and historical sources and their cinematic repetitions? And, how have they changed in the course of cinematic history? The second: Why *Psycho*, *Carmen* and *Joan of Arc*? What drives the "mental machinery" of cinema to present the same stories over and over again? What hidden features cause the public to repeatedly consume them? And is there a possible connection between cinematic repetition and collective trauma?

Structure and Content

As repetitions involving constants and variations, multi-versions posit themselves against the grain of both history and the language of cinema. The first chapter, "Inside and Outside the Frame," introduces and discusses the ritual dimension of repetition from an institutional point of view. Working within the framework of a particular genre, the chain of Psycho is used here as a musical key exhibiting the dominant mode of operation that characterizes visual and cinematic repetition in its relation to the practices of pleasure. The concluding chapter, " Repetitions as Hidden Streams," reassesses the hierarchical relations between the cinematic machinery as a sub-system within the larger field of cultural production, and suggests a typology for understanding the various modes of repetition that operate in cinema.

The core of the book deals with the Carmen and Joan of Arc chains of repetition, and is divided into two parts, each comprising three parallel chapters. Part One deals with Carmen and Part Two with Joan of Arc. The chains of repetitions are posited as two variations, mirroring each other:

Part One includes three successive chapters, "The Game Begins," "Muted Voices" and "Masks." The first examines how we see a *constant* when given a *variable* (to rephrase Hofstadter). The issue of adaptations versus multi-versions will be presented in order to identify versions in the context of "family resemblance." Exploring the aesthetic and cultural trajectories of a cinematic chain like Carmen, I discuss its official and unofficial sources and the multiplicity of variations. The discussion covers the ground from Mérimée and Bizet (19th century) to cinematic versions from DeMille (1915) to MTV and Robert Townsend's

Carmen Hip Hopera (2001). "Muted Voices" traces the various rewritings of one of the most significant elements in the corpus – Carmen's first aria, the *Haba-ñera*. A comparative reading of the *Carmen* cinematic chain vis-à-vis the chain of Manet's *Olympia* (1865) produces a social narrative in which differences and similarities are exposed. "Masks," re-reads the *Carmen* story as a fantasy of control and follows the trope of smuggling; In many cinematic *Carmen* texts the gesture of smuggling functions in dissimilar ethnic masks as a repetitive practice, encapsulating the presence of the Romani in a cinematic forbidden space.

Part Two, dealing with Joan of Arc, also comprises three chapters: "The Game Again," "Hearing Voices," and "Disguises". "The Game Again" introduces the relations between sources and variations that are much more complicated than in Carmen because, as a historical biographical film, it attempts to recreate a reality that no longer exists. The key to understanding the eternal ritual of repetition can perhaps be found in the story's genealogy, which has produced the myth as it is told and retold, first by Joan's testimonies and then by those who recorded and interpreted them. "Hearing Voices" focuses on the changing dynamic between filmic material, generic conventions and historical knowledge: Joan's "voices" contribute to her otherness and constitute one of the most significant and yet enigmatic details in both her career and in the historical myth. "Disguises" tries to measure the borders of version, and to explore further the role of disguises in a chain of multi-versions that includes A MAGGOT (John Fowles, 1985), ALIEN III (David Fincher, 1992) and BREAKING THE WAVES (Lars von Trier, 1996). These disguised versions tell us about the possibly devious ways in which the texts have circumvented social and cultural rules of censorship.

In this book, the combination of cultural, filmic and theoretical materials unfolds as a virtual game – a game of repetition and variation.

Note

1. According to *CinémAction* 1989 (53): 28-32 and James L.Limbacher,1991. For the versions of the Carmen story, see the list in Protopopoff 1989 (53): 55-63 and also in *Cinematographe* 52 *Dossier Cinéma et Opéra* 1979: 128-29. Interestingly enough, the two sources are not identical and list different items. There is a Carmen Project in progress at the University of Newcastle upon Tyne and according to their findings there are no less than 77 versions, but this data also includes recordings of the opera. It is possible that additional versions of the Carmen story exist. For the versions of the Joan story see the list in *Les Cahiers de la Cinémathèque: Reuve d'histoire du Cinéma* (*Le Moyen Age au Cinéma*) no. 42/43: 39 with the addition of Herzog's & Cheetham's 1990 version, Rivette 1993 and Besson 1999. According to electronic sources the numbers are even higher (IMDb, Cinemania, and BFI index, 2002).

Chapter 1
PSYCHO: Inside and Outside the Frame

The cinematic medium, by virtue of its technology, encapsulates 24 versions of potential movement per second. Within the same shot, each frame is an earlier version of the frame about to be seen. Seriality is constitutive in the very material of the cinema, i.e., its film strip. The cinema's "self-differing" elements might be identified as its specificity (Krauss, 2000: 44) but its differences are countered in favor of continuity during the screening process (Bellour, 1979; Baudry, 1985 [1970]; Usai, 2001).[1] A parallel process of difference, repetition and denial also exists in the cinema's imaginary archive. This imaginary archive exists in the spectator's mind and is comprised of all the texts that have been absorbed, thus enabling the production of a network of comparisons among them.[2] One of the significant undercurrents of cinematic history is that of serial repetitions and their variations, so often overlooked. It is my intention to slow down the flow of new films and new data and trace one of the most persistent serial repetitions in the history of cinema.

When we talk of series of repetitions in any medium, however, we have to distinguish between auto-repetition, which is controlled and highly conscious, and cultural repetition which is not always conscious, certainly not controlled, and occurs in the public domain outside of "lab-controlled" conditions. Auto-repetition can be exemplified by Andy Warhol's series of paintings of Marilyn Monroe (1962, 1964, 1979-1986) or the Campbell's soup tins (1962, 1968, 1970), by Hitchcock's own remake of THE MAN WHO KNEW TOO MUCH (the first in 1943 with Edna Best and Leslie Banks and the second in 1954 with Doris Day and James Stewart) or by Tom Tykwer's LOLA RENNT (RUN LOLA RUN) in 1998.[3] Cultural repetition, on the other hand, the rewriting of the same text that may or may not be conscious but is not entirely controlled, can be illustrated by the many repetitions and variations of the Cinderella story (e.g., MOONSTRUCK, PRETTY WOMAN), the *Romeo and Juliet* story (WEST SIDE STORY), or Manet's *Olympia*.[4] This latter, "wild" type of repetition in cinema and art involves not only issues of repetition and variation but also the issue of the collective subconscious of a particular society or culture, which results in the continued repetition of certain texts. It is my contention that all of these stories are encoded expressions that society keeps transforming in order to tell itself about itself. The constant repetition of the same stories, like the retelling of myths in the sense to which Lévi-Strauss referred (1958), keeps them alive in social memory, continually transmitting their meaning and relevance.

What, then, are the cultural and aesthetic functions of repetitive texts and their mechanisms? What characterizes the repetitive appearance of a certain story? And what kinds of images have been projected again and again over long periods of time?

"Vertical inquiry" is the term used by Maya Deren to describe the character-istic feature of both poetry and experimental films (1953). It is the ramification of the moment – the illumination of moments as they appear – in such a way that a concatenation of such illuminated moments results. According to the lo-gic of the "ramification of the moment," as I suggest we read it, it is not only the appearance of one specific film that has to be explored but its genealogy as well. Thus, the presence of a specific story, myth or theme and its ramifications could be read not only within the context of a genre, a period, an *auteur* or a medium, but also as a multifaceted cultural praxis.

In order to present the logic of repetition as both an intertextual and a ritual act, I will trace through a selected chain of repetitions: (a) cinema as a sub-sys-tem of a culture that both affects and is affected by that culture; (b) the dy-namics of repetition; and (c) the "pleasure principle" behind the obstinate reap-pearance of certain stories and myths down through the history of cinema. By using the case of PSYCHO, which works within the framework of a particular genre, I will explore the dominant mode of operation that characterizes visual and cinematic repetition in its relation to the practices of pleasure. PSYCHO re-volves around "the gaze" upon a woman and her death as one of its main tropes. By its repetitions and variations, the film delineates a visual and narra-tive regime in which feminine/masculine relations are inscribed and controlled.

The Cinematic Institution

In order to understand the mechanism of repetition I would suggest that we identify it as part of the activity of what is known as the "cinematic institution." The cinematic institution, a theoretical construct, presupposes that films do not exist in a vacuum: they are conceived, produced, distributed and consumed within specific economic and social contexts (Kochberg, 1996: 14). In this sense, it is a system that maintains the medium as a socio-cultural activity, much as painting, literature or pop music, for example, are also maintained. As part of the hegemonic culture of a given society, it also determines who and what will be remembered by the community for a longer period of time.[5] Cinematic repe-tition can thus be understood as impressing the "fingerprints" of the cinematic institution on its relationship with other cultural, social and aesthetic systems and reflecting the cinematic institution's system of preferences, thus habituating the viewer to certain habits of spectatorship.

The act of repetition is performed both by the sender (the cinematic institution) and by the receiver (the audience) – who is ready to consume the same or a similar product again and again – and it is anchored in the selection of the texts being repeated. Using Pierre Bourdieu's notion of "the market of symbolic goods," that is, the cultural assets or resources of a society (1971), we can say that any given society has a tendency to choose certain symbolic goods over others. The "symbolic goods" of the cinema are marketed, for example, by film festivals, distributors, newspapers, video shops, internet sites, critics' choices published periodically in film magazines, television shows, histories of the cinema dealing with films according to periods, directors or genres, and – we must end somewhere – by promotional and educational systems.[6] This variety of activity contributes to the delineation of the ever-changing coordinates of the canonic repertoire of the cinematic institution. The production of cultural goods, however, is always organized according to demands present in the given society but outside the specific systems themselves. Most of them reflect the deep subliminal desires and fears that shape each particular human *habitus*. The term is taken from zoology and refers to the interior environment acquired in the course of the collective history or milieu of a species, the paradigms of its identity and preferences. According to Bourdieu (1977, 1990), *habitus* is a "socialized subjectivity" i.e., a system of dispositions acquired or adopted in a given milieu under the constraints of the prevailing formation of relations to a certain field.[7] And, Bourdieu adds: "… agents merely need to let themselves follow their own social 'nature,' that is, what history has made of them, to be as it were, 'naturally' adjusted to the historical world they are up against …" (Bourdieu, 1990: 90, in John H. Scahill, 1993).

In this sense we may understand Christian Metz's observation about the cinema as an industry that internalizes norms of spectatorship: "The cinematic institution is not just the cinema industry (which works to fill cinemas, not to empty them); it is also the *mental machinery* – another industry – which spectators 'accustomed to cinema' have internalized" (1975: 7, emphasis added).[8]

If we consider the cinematic institution as a kind of *habitus*, which functions in order to shape and reshape the spectators' taste, habits and preferences, we can then recognize the institutional function of specific repetitions as symptomatic. In this context, I would like to follow some of the theoretical assumptions of both the Formalist tradition and Itamar Even-Zohar's *polysystem* theory (1990), and to replace the question of "How aesthetics and cultural norms function in principle?" by "How do aesthetic and cultural norms function along the time axis?"[9] Telling the histories of the cinematic chains of PSYCHO, *Carmen* and *Joan of Arc* in terms of constants and variations enables the present study to identify cinematic repetition as a responsive element within a hierarchical structure, and to demonstrate how the cinematic institution maintains a mutual relationship with the cultural system at large.

The Dynamic of Repetitions

Hitchcock's PSYCHO was first released in 1960 and became a landmark within the horror genre.[10] Three sequels have thus far been made to PSYCHO: by Richard Franklin (1983), Anthony Perkins (1986) and Mick Garris (1990).[11] In 1998 Gus Van Sant made a remake and declared it a homage to PSYCHO. Homage was also paid to PSYCHO with pastiches like Tobe Hooper's TEXAS CHAINSAW MASSACRE (1974), John Carpenter's HALLOWEEN (1974) and Brian de Palma's DRESSED TO KILL (1980).[12] To these one might add the video installation made by Douglas Gordon, 24 HOUR PSYCHO (1993). The numerous writings or rewritings of PSYCHO will enable us to trace the dynamics of repetition within the framework of the horror genre, which operate within and vis-à-vis mainstream cinematic conventions. Moreover, it is part and parcel of a much broader discourse and testifies to the interrelations between cinema and culture at large. The remakes, the sequels, and even the trailers all participate in a pleasurable game of repetition which has contributed to turning the film into a fetish. Any remake of a film is, according to Umberto Eco, the retelling of a previously successful story (Eco, 1985: 167). Since repetition and difference function in mutual interdependence, the economy of cinematic versions is that of difference in repetition. In this tension, I believe, lies the secret of the eternal charm of cinematic remakes.

It is my intention to deal with PSYCHO on two levels. First of all to examine the dynamics of repetition (and pleasure) as exemplified by a comparison of the opening sequences in Hitchcock's original with those in Van Sant's 1998 remake. Then to have another look at the central element in the film, the shower scene, which contributed to establish PSYCHO as a cult film and fetish.

Viewing the rewriting of PSYCHO, whether as sequel or remake, involves a dialectic interplay between old and new, innovation and repetition.[13] With Gus Van Sant's official remake of the film in 1998, however, the interplay reached a new extreme. According to Jacques Lacan (1977, in Neale 1980: 50), "repetition demands the new," yet Universal Studios claimed that Van Sant's PSYCHO was a line-by-line, shot-by-shot duplication of Hitchcock's – except for unavoidable differences in casting and color.[14] *Variety* has trouble categorizing the film:

Imitation, in the case of Gus Van Sant's "Psycho," may be the sincerest form of flattery, but it's hardly the most scintillating. A faithful-unto-slavish remake of the 1960 Hitchcock classic pic contains nothing to outrage or offend partisans of the original, yet neither does it stand to add much to their appreciation (Godfrey Cheshire, 1998, in *Variety*).

The opening sequence of Hitchcock's PSYCHO achieves a restless graphic and rhythmic quality through Bernard Herrmann's music and the lines which violently crisscross the screen as the titles deliver the credits. The title of the film, PSYCHO, appears in its now-famous font, breaking in two, portending, perhaps, the schizophrenic personality of Norman Bates. "Phoenix, Arizona" says the title screened on the background of an urban landscape photographed in black and white like the rest of the film. A horizontal camera movement slowly zooms in to the window of a hotel room. "Friday, December 11" is announced by the inter-title, followed by "2: 43 p.m." Dilapidated Venetian blinds indicate the tawdriness of the hotel where Marion (Janet Leigh) is spending an afternoon with her boyfriend Sam (John Gavin). In the bedroom, half dressed, Marion is telling Sam who is already dressed that they can no longer meet this way. She wants a respectable relationship. (See ill. V a)

The opening sequence of Van Sant's PSYCHO maintains the jumpy graphic and rhythmic qualities of Hitchcock's opening sequence. Along green lines which crisscross the screen the credits appear. When the title of the film appears, it splits in two. The camera captures an urban landscape (in color) and then zooms slowly into the hotel room where Marion (Anne Heche) is spending the afternoon with her boyfriend (Viggo Mortenson). "Phoenix, Arizona," appears, then "Friday, December 11," and then "1998."[15] And, finally, "2: 43 p.m." Van Sant echoes Hitchcock in providing the time and place and in the way the fonts jump onto the screen. The dialogue seems to be identical, although this time the scene begins with the couple lying in bed in their underwear and Marion saying that they cannot meet this way anymore. She wants a respectable relationship.[16] (See ill. V b)

Palimpsestos (palimpsest) is the Greek word for a parchment upon which one text has been superimposed upon another in such a way that the old writing may be partly visible through the new. The palimpsest already enfolds within itself the dialectic of repetition, the dialectic of old and new, before and after, the desire to re-view the same story and the pleasure of its realization. Repetition here is firstly a movement in time: "re-take," "re-turn," "re-verse" and "re-write" – all of which involve looking back at what existed before (Melberg 1990: 74). Since the makeover of some of the details depends largely on the time gap between the 1960s and the 1990s and thus, for the most, updates the atmosphere, the differences between Hitchcock's writing and Van Sant's overwriting seem to result from a mechanical transformation.[17] Is it necessary, then, to be familiar with Hitchcock's version in order to enjoy Van Sant's?

In his discussion of repetition in mass culture, Umberto Eco enumerates three necessary phases: "(1) Something is offered as original and different (according to the requirements of modern aesthetics); (2) we are aware that this something is repeating something else that we already know; and (3) notwithstanding this – better just because of it – we like it (and buy it)" (Eco, 1985: 167). Interestingly, Eco differentiates between modernist and postmodernist repetitions. According to *modernist aesthetics,* he points out, every good work of art must conform to the dialectic between scheme and innovation. *Postmodernist aesthetics,* on the other hand, is interested less in the single variation than in variation *ad infinitum* as a formal principle.[18] In this sense, Van Sant's text is an example of postmodernist aesthetics and it is in this context that we can understand Slavoj Žižek's observations. While dealing with the ideal remake for Hitchcock, for example, he says:

> The idea of the exact frame-by-frame remake is an ingenious idea, and, in my view, the problem was rather that the film did not go far enough in this direction. Ideally, what the film should strive for is to achieve the uncanny effect of the double: in shooting formally the same film, the difference would have became all the more palpable – everything would have been the same, same shots, angles, dialogue, and, nonetheless, on account of this very sameness, we would all the more powerfully experience that we are dealing with a totally different film (2001: 12).[19]

It would seem that Van Sant's text needs an ideal spectator – one who is familiar with and recognizes Hitchcock's text. Working within the conventions of postmodernist aesthetics, this experience plays on the "spectator's horizon of expectations" for a new kind of variation. But there is actually nothing "new" here – save the movement of "repetition" itself. However, this aesthetic experience is also a cultural one due to the special status of Psycho as a cult film. [20]

Psycho, Fetishism and Pleasure

> "Fetish? You name it. All I know is that I've always had to
> have it with me."
> David Bloch, *The Scarf*[21]

The critical discourse on Psycho – in film reviews, journals and books, in audience reactions, the spate of imitations, the production of soundtracks and in the development of a trivia industry around the film – points unambiguously to "the shower scene" as the key to its enduring quality as cult film or fetish.[22] Surprisingly, or perhaps not, Hitchcock himself was the first to evaluate the shower scene as a cardinal one. In the trailer for PSYCHO, prepared and narrated by Hitchcock himself, he says:

> The bathroom. Oh, they've cleaned all this up now. Big difference. You should have seen the blood. [...] Well, the murderer, you see, crept in here very silently – of course the shower was on, there was no sound, and ...[23]

This is followed by a shot of the shower curtain. Structured like a guided tour on location where "horrible events took place," the trailer introduces the viewer to the Bates Motel, the house nearby with a staircase and bedroom and, most importantly, a bathroom. The tour culminates behind the shower curtain where the viewer is surprised to see Janet Leigh making horrible grimaces, with loud, scary, rhythmic music in the background.[24] Towards the end of the trailer, before entering the bathroom, Hitchcock calls the viewers' attention to the presence of a painting hanging on the wall. The painting camouflages the hole in the wall through which Norman will peep at Marion while she gets ready for her shower. "By the way," Hitchcock says, "this picture has great significance because ... let's go along." And the viewer remains wondering what the significance of the painting is. The painting is one of the many versions of *Susanna and the Elders*. At the center of the composition is a naked woman in a defensive posture, embarrassed by the erotic gaze of two old men who have penetrated her privacy. Through the mechanism of intertextual activity, the painting prefigures the violent act of rape/murder that will take place on screen.[25]

In her study *Feminism in Art History* (1982), Mary Garrard finds that

> ... few artistic themes have offered so satisfying an opportunity for legitimized voyeurism as *Susanna and the Elders*. The subject was taken up with relish by artists from the sixteenth through eighteenth centuries as an opportunity to display the feminine nude, in much the same spirit that such themes as Danae or Lucretia were approached, but with the added advantage that the nude's erotic appeal could be heightened by the presence of the two lecherous old men, whose inclusion was both iconographically justified and pornographically effective (ibid.: 149-150, quoted in Martin Lefebvre, 1997: 136).[26]

William Rothman (1982) echoes this kind of spectatorship experience in relation to PSYCHO:

> Our views of Marion constitute her as a sexual object. [...] Our views of Marion awaken an appetite that cannot be satisfied by more views, but only by transcending the act of viewing as such. [...] Our pleasure in viewing Marion cannot be separated from

our fantasy that we are about to possess her sexually. [...] Ours is a fantasy of rape (ibid.: 295-296).[27]

The film itself signals the importance of the shower scene by its cinematic language: the special editing work consists of over *90 cuts in two minutes and 53 seconds*! As described by David Sterritt (1993):

> And then Marion gets killed, in the most celebrated montage of Hitchcock's career. Its most significant aspect may be the fact that its kineticism not only shows but obscures. That is, [...] we [...] feel confused as to what's exactly going on, except in the general sense that Marion is being knifed to death" (ibid.: 108).

This scene has a crucial function in the narrative as well. The murder of the heroine takes place in the middle of the film. Robin Wood has described it as follows: "When it is over, and she is dead, we are left shocked, with nothing to cling to, the apparent center of the film entirely dissolved" (1965: 118). This is a narrative structure that changed the rules of the genre.[28] The heroine has been removed from the story right in the middle of it. The second part of the movie is an attempt to trace back the actions which led to the "premature" climax and to understand them. By looking back to its beginnings, the second part of the film actually rewrites the first part, positioning the shower scene at dead center. Like Eurydice before her, Marion lost her life because of a male fantasy, encapsulated in his gaze upon her. The man looked where he should not have looked and the rest of the text will deal with the consequences of this forbidden look.

In the course of time, this scene was singled out by viewers and they tried to evoke it again and again. What can be referred to as the reception space, that is, the cultural environment, embraced PSYCHO and endowed it with a "cult" status, complete with quotations, allusions, homages and direct and indirect transformations. In this ritual, Hitchcock's film was acknowledged as the original text, while its sources of inspiration were overlooked. They include the novel by Robert Bloch (1959), which in turn was inspired by a true story that appeared in the *Weyauwega Chronicle* (Rebello, 1998: 8). Another source, suggested at the Hitchcock exhibition in Paris (*Hitchcock et l'art: coincidences fatales*, 2001, held at the Pompidou), might be Fritz Lang's scene from WHILE THE CITY SLEEPS (1956) which bears an astonishing resemblance to the murder scene in PSYCHO. Hitchcock's film, however, has acquired the status of the "original" – everything else is an imitation.

The aura of the work of art – which according to Walter Benjamin (1969 [1936]) has been lost with the mechanical reproduction of work of art – seems to be restored by the way the film and the murder scene are represented both inside and outside of movie theaters. At the Hitchcock exhibition in Paris, for example, in a darkened hall and against the background of Bernard Herrmann's music, significant objects from his films are exhibited on red velvet inside of glass cases, like expensive jewelry. In one of the cases, visitors can see Marion's "original" bra, with a note indicating its source: PSYCHO.[29] At Universal Studios in Los Angeles, one can visit "the bathroom from the Bates Motel," with its souvenirs of towels and soap, and experience thus the blurring of boundaries between PSYCHO "as text" and PSYCHO "as event" (according to Elsaesser's distinction, 2001)

The "shower scene," for example, has been rewritten in Brian de Palma's DRESSED TO KILL (both in the elevator scene and prior to the film's dénoument). It is also suggested in a cartoon featuring "The Simpsons," and in the soundtrack on the PSYCHO web site.[30] Interestingly, the reception space, which surrounds Hitchcock's film, redefines its emblematic essence again and again, acknowledging the cultural status of the scene but also contributing to its fetishistic aura. By evoking metonymically the whole film through the "shower scene," cinematic and cultural institutions contribute to the cumulative effect that identifies the film with the voyeuristic fantasy. [31]

(Sources)
Various artists *Susanna and the Elders*
(unofficial) Fritz Lang (1956) WHILE THE CITY SLEEPS
(official) Robert Bloch (1959) PSYCHO

|

Alfred Hitchcock (1960) PSYCHO

|

(Sequels)
Richard Franklin (1983) PSYCHO II
Anthony Perkins (1986) PSYCHO III
Mick Garris (1990) PSYCHO IV

|

(Homages, versions)
Brian de Palma (1980) DRESSED TO KILL [32]
Douglas Gordon (1993) 24 HOUR PSYCHO
Gus Van Sant (1998) PSYCHO

Figure 1: *Psycho's Genealogy*

Mary Garrard, in her study of paintings depicting the Old Testament story of Susanna and the elders (Daniel: 13, Vulgate version), describes the ways in which the genre of female nudity produces "legitimized voyeurism" (1982: 149). As John Berger shows, Western artists have reified women by making them a spectacle. In *Ways of Seeing*, Berger argues that "women have been seen and judged as sights" (1978: 57). Cinema works within this scopic regime, continually representing men "surveying" women and women "being surveyed." Laura Mulvey, in her seminal essay (1975), identifies this "position" in mainstream cinema, describing it in terms of the dominant male gaze at the woman: she exists only "to be looked at."[33] The woman who looks back (as in Manet's *Olympia*) denies her passivity and signals knowledge and vision, not only visibility.[34] *Susanna and the Elders*, once again, might exemplify the revealing/concealing dynamic of woman's awareness of her status as spectacle. The paintings of the story of Susanna use various practices to organize *her* gaze, thus systematically avoiding her looking back: Susanna looks at herself and indirectly at the viewer through the mirror (Tintoretto), at the two elders located above or behind her (Rubens, Rembrandt, Carracci), or down, her eyes almost closed (Cantarini). The series of paintings of the Susanna story focus on the sexual harassment of a married woman by two conspiring and influential men of the community. According to the Old Testament, the men have threatened to testify against her if she does not consent to their advances and she declares her readiness to die rather than be abused. At her trial Daniel testifies to and proves her innocence. Western art, however, has seen fit to preserve and deliver only the voyeuristic scene, completely ignoring the heroic aspect of Susanna's role in the story.

PSYCHO's fantasy of control has become a fetish in a culture in which the myth of *Orpheus and Eurydice* also has pride of place. Dating back to antiquity and the writings of Ovid and Virgil, and continuing through the works of Politian, Paul Valery, Victor Hugo, Guillaume Apollinaire and Tennessee Williams, the films by Jean Cocteau (1950, 1959) and Marcel Camus (1958), among many others, the myth has been rewritten again and again.[35] As noted by Pierre Brunel, Orpheus's gaze is upon an already-lost Eurydice, who is found again and lost again (2001: 42). The gaze that results in the loss is the absolute minimal unit of the myth. What would the story of *Orpheus* be without his turning back to look at Eurydice as they return from Hades (Blanchot: 1955)? But we could also say, what would the story of Hitchcock's VERTIGO (1958) be without Scotty's look at Judy/Madeleine? Or Edgar Allen Poe's painter in *Oval Picture* "looking" his model to death? Or Godard's look at Nana in VIVRE SA VIE? The defining element of all these stories is the male gaze, a gaze that heralds the narrative's denouement and the death of the woman, the passive victim of his fantasy.[36]

By means of concealment and denial, serial repetitions turn the repeated object (painting, story) into a stereotyped fetish. In this way, cultural institutions domesticate the chosen object by turning it into one that evokes only pleasure. The chosen object always contains unresolved, disturbing elements which society seeks to exorcize.

Within the cultural context of this tradition, I would like to posit the cinematic chains of *Carmen* and *Joan of Arc*, each of which might be described here as a "reverse shot" of both *Susanna and the Elders* and PSYCHO.

Looking through the imaginary archive of the cinema, we may note the presence of specific repetitions, which, however persistent, remain outside the scope of the main frame. Crossing the familiar institutional boundaries of genre, stars or period, *Carmen* and *Joan of Arc* have accumulated an increasing number of cinematic versions – over 50 of the Carmen story and 40 of the Joan story to date. The fact that both stories deal with exceptional female heroines who challenge social laws and die as a result suggests that what underlies these numerous retellings is what Jameson calls "social narrative" – coded expressions of society's norms.

Thomas Elsaesser's observations (2001) regarding blockbuster films are significant in this respect. While discussing the repetitive structure of the blockbuster Elsaesser identifies two main features:

> First, a big subject and a big budget (world war, disaster, end of planet, monster from the deep, holocaust, death battle in the galaxy). Second, a young male hero, usually with lots of firepower, or secret knowledge, or an impossibly difficult mission. The big movie is necessarily based on traditional stories, sometimes against the background of historical events, more often a combination of fantasy or sci-fi, with the well known archetypal heroes from Western mythology on parade (ibid.: 16-17).

Versions of *Carmen* and *Joan* are sometimes, but not necessarily, big-budget productions. Sometimes they work against the background of historical events (mainly in the case of *Joan*), but Carmen and Joan are both archetypal, and distinctly feminine, *heroines* of Western mythology who thus operate against the traditional binarism that aims to locate feminine identities within already established frames. As we shall see, these exceptional chains function both within and outside of the visual regime, challenging its borders.

Following Gilles Deleuze's observation that "repetition is pathos and the philosophy of repetition is pathology" (1994 [1968]: 290), we may identify these chains of repetition and variations as symptoms of those areas over which the master narrative has lost control. These are the primordial unknown, the terrifying and disturbing holes which culture has to clarify (in Alice Jardine's words [1985]). Through endless repetitions, the cinematic institution is relentlessly trying to reframe the non-frameable. And if by way of repetition the object in the mainstream is not only repeated but re-designed according to the prevailing norms of society, does repetition succeed also in taming repeated objects – such as Joan and Carmen – that are outside the mainstream?

Notes

1. In "Cine-Repetitions" (1979) Raymond Bellour remarks that: "Repetition is internal when it pertains to the very body of the film, to its most elementary and paradoxical level: that of the single frame ... An endless repetition, twenty-four times per second" (ibid: 66).

2. I am following and developing here André Malroux's term (1951) "musée imaginaire" in a similar way to that suggested by Martin Lefebvre while discussing sequels as a series (1997, 163-166).

3. The last example RUN LOLA RUN is exception in the sense that it is an internal repetition (see Bellour's distinction, 1979) which presents three variations of the same story in the film.

4. See also the discussion on *Olympia* in Chapter 3.

5. "It is the institution which governs the norms prevailing in this activity, sanctioning some and rejecting others" (Even-Zohar, 1990: 36). See also Bourdieu, 1979, and Noël Carroll, 1996.

6. A well-known example of evaluating symbolic goods would be Andrew Sarris's book *The American Cinema: Directors and Directions, 1929-1968* (1968). In order to identify "the trees" in "the forest of cinema," he has classified films according to *auteurs,* running the gamut from the "pantheon of cinema" to "less than meets the eye."

7. See Even-Zohar 1990 [1979] and John Scahill (1993).

8. Cited in Neale, 1980: 19.

9. In Itamar Even-Zohar 1990 (1979) and Brian McHale: 1987: 6-7. And McHale adds: "To describe change of dominant is in effect to describe the process of (literary) historical change" (1987: 7). In this context see also Steve Neale on the genre (1991).

10. See, for example, Noël Carroll, 1998 (1982).

11. Which is in effect a "prequel" (called PSYCHO IV: THE BEGINNING). These are declared sequels. Many more unofficial sequels have been made with titles such as PSYCHO LOVER by Robert Vincent O'Neill (1970), PSYCHO SISTERS by Pete Jacelone (1978) or MOTOR PSYCHO by Alex Downs (1992).

12. See David Bordwell's discussion of the critical discourse around PSYCHO, "Rhetoric in Action: Seven Models of PSYCHO" (1989: 235). See also Vera Dika for a discussion of THE TEXAS CHAINSAW MASSACRE and the reception of PSYCHO as a subgenre (2003: 66-78).

13. As observed by McDougal (1998) while writing about the Hitchcock autoremake THE MAN WHO KNEW TOO MUCH (1934, 1955): "The notion of a remake becomes complex with a filmmaker like Hitchcock, who was continuously and obsessively remaking his own work" (ibid: 52).

14. In Thomas Leitch (2000: 269). William Rothman has also remarked that "Van Sant's film reminds us – as if we needed reminding – that we are to take with a grain of salt Hitchcock's remarks to the effect that his creative work was finished before filming began [...]" (1999: 29).
15. As noted by Leitch (1998), Van Sant adds the year to the date over the opening shot.
16. See Barbara Klinger's analysis of the beginning and ending of the film (1982), and Bordwell on Klinger (1989: 239-241)
17. As has been observed by Leitch (2000) there are at least 101 differences between Hitchcock's film and Van Sant's.
18. Consequently, as Eco claims, unlike its status in previous periods, repetition in the twentieth century belongs equally to popular and high culture.
19. Žižek begins this observation by saying that: "Gus van Sant's Psycho [...] I am inclined to consider a failed masterpiece, rather than a simple failure" (ibid).
20. Leitch, in his definition of homage, defines it as a remake meant to honor the original, rather than the pretension of being better than the original (1990).
21. In Rebello (1998: 8).
22. Space limits the possibility of discussing or even presenting here the enormous amount of material on Psycho. In this sense, David Bordwell's discussion of seven models of the film (1989) is a meta-discourse that illustrates some milestones in the long and rich history of Psycho criticism till 1989.
23. My transcription of the trailer.
24. According to Rebello (1998: 155) the shrieking woman in the trailer is none other than Vera Miles (Marion's sister) in a wig.
25. It is worth mentioning here that numerous variations of *Susanna and the Elders* exist, among them those of Tintoretto (1555-56), Guido Reni (1620) Annibale Carracci (1590), Artemisia Gentileschi (1610), Guernico (1617), Anthony Van Dyck (1621-22), Peter Paul Rubens (1636-40), Simone Cantarini (1640-42), and Rembrandt van Rijn (1647) as well as various anonymous artists.
26. Both Martin Lefebvre (1997) and Donald Spoto (2001) suggest a cultural explanation of this picture in relation to feminist discourse.
27. Rothman continues, albeit in parentheses: "If this is a male fantasy, it is not one that only men in Hitchcock's audience may indulge. For men and women among the film's viewers, the act of viewing possesses both active and passive aspects, call them 'masculine' and 'feminine.'"
28. See Noël Carroll on Psycho and the genre of horror film (1990).
29. Another case exhibits the mother's skull.
30. Homer Simpson accidentally falls down in the bathroom. At the same time a tin can falls and red liquid pours out, graphically imitating the main lines of composition of the murder scene in Psycho, testifying to the stature of the bathroom scene in our culture.
31. For a discussion of the film commodity as legitimized voyeurism, especially in regard to the blockbuster phenomenon, see Thomas Elsaesser (2001: 15). On fetishization as eternalization see Kenneth Marc Harris (1992).
32. The substantial presence of references and allusions to Hithcock's film in Dressed to Kill creates an analogy between the two texts on various levels. These interrelations enable me to define it as "a version" and not only as an allusion, as defined by

Noël Carroll (1998 [1982]: 249). See also Chapter 5 for definitions of intertextual relationships.

33. As demonstrated by Linda Williams, 2002 (1983), in the genre of the horror film the woman's active gaze is ultimately punished.

34. See Mary Ann Doane (1982: 82). John Berger argues that the woman as a spectator is split into "a surveyor" and "a surveyed." She is constantly aware of being looked at even as she herself gazes. In film studies, Mary Ann Doane makes a distinction, while describing woman as spectacle rather than spectator, between primary and secondary identifications in these procedure of seeing (Linda Williams, in Jancovich, 2002: 65-66).

35. See also Pierre Brunel (2001).

36. See also Elizabeth Bronfen, *No End to Her* (1996 [1992]).

Part One

First Variation: Carmen

Chapter 2
The Game Begins

In CARMEN JONES (1954) Otto Preminger transferred the plot of Georges Bizet's opera *Carmen* from Spain to the United States of the 1950s, while Oscar Hammerstein adapted the music. Joe, a young black army officer replaces Don José, Cindy-Lou is Micaëla, Haskey, the boxer, replaces the toreador, and the boxing-ring replaces the *corrida*. Carmen Jones, who works in an army canteen, is none other than the Carmen of Prosper Mérimée and Bizet.[1] Another variation, Jean-Luc Godard's PRÉNOM CARMEN (1983), revolves around a Carmen who robs a bank in order to finance a film production for her uncle, Jean, a former director and her guardian.[2] Joseph, her partner in crime, is Don José, while Dennis, the script-writer and Joseph's rival for Carmen's heart, has been substituted for the toreador in the story. Claire, the musician, is the other woman in this Carmen/Joseph triangle.

As manifest versions of *Carmen*, these two films exhibit different transformations of plot, character and location. In what sense, then, can we conclude, along with Jeremy Tambling (1987: 27), that "there is no *Carmen* or Carmen: there are simply re-surfacings of a similar situation where the names encourage a false sense of continuity"? I will argue that the logic of multiple cinematic versions resides, first of all, in the special features of the text that are repeated and, secondly, in the dynamic between the constant and variable elements. The question that remains, however, is: how do we see a *constant* given a *variable* (to paraphrase Hofstadter (1985b [1982])), and by the same token, how do we perceive variability given constancy?

Ever since the publication of Prosper Mérimée's novella in 1845, and the production of Georges Bizet's opera in 1875, *Carmen* has had a lasting presence in opera, theater and dance, as well as in dozens of films, and even, recently, in computer games.[3] By repeating the story again and again – either à la Mérimée or à la Bizet or, as in most versions, as a variation of the two – culture has kept the myth circulating in society's bloodstream, signaling its continued relevance.[4] *Carmen* is not only one of the all-time favorites of opera-goers but one of the cinematic institution's highly preferred subjects for production, re-production, rewrites and remakes.[5]

Over fifty film versions of the Carmen story have been produced to date. They include the notable films of Cecil B. DeMille (CARMEN, USA, 1915); Charlie

Chaplin (A BURLESQUE ON CARMEN, USA, 1916); Ernst Lubitsch (CARMEN/ GYPSY BLOOD, Germany, 1918); Maurits H. Binger and Hans Nesna (EEN CARMEN VAN HET NOORDEN/A CARMEN OF THE NORTH, the Netherlands, 1919); Jacques Feyder (CARMEN, France, 1926); Raoul Walsh (CARMEN, USA, 1915; THE LOVES OF CARMEN, USA, 1927); Cecil Lewis (CARMEN, UK, 1931); Lotte Reiniger (CARMEN, Germany, 1933); Victor Janson (DIE BLONDE CARMEN/ THE BLONDE CARMEN, Germany, 1935); Anson Dyer (CARMEN, UK, 1936); Christian-Jaque, (CARMEN, France, 1942-45); Luis César Amadori (CARMEN, Argentine, 1943); Charles Vidor (THE LOVES OF CARMEN, USA, 1948); Keiske Kinoshita (KARUMEN KOKYO NI KAERU/ CARMEN COMES HOME, Japan, 1951); Otto Preminger (CARMEN JONES, USA, 1954); Tulio Demaicheli (LA CARMEN DE RONDA /CARMEN FROM GRANADE, Spain, 1959); Carlos Saura (CARMEN, Spain, 1983), Jean-Luc Godard (PRÉNOM CARMEN/ FIRST NAME: CARMEN, France, 1983); Peter Brook (LA TRAGÉDIE DE CARMEN/ CARMEN'S TRAGEDY, UK & France, 1984); Francesco Rosi (CARMEN, Italy, 1984); Makoto Sato and Akira Sugiura (CARMEN, Japan, 1989) and, more recently, Joseph Gaï Ramaka (KARMEN GEÏ/CARMEN, Senegal & France, 2001); Robert Townsend's MTV CARMEN: A HIP HOPERA (USA, 2001); and Vicente Aranda (CARMEN, Spain, 2003). (I have not included videotapes and filmic recordings of operatic performances in this count.)

In my discussion of the chain of Carmen repetitions, I will deal in this chapter primarily with the act of repetition itself, that is, with the relations that exist, first, between "source" and versions and, then, among the versions themselves. I will examine a few concepts and their potential for illuminating the existing relations between source and multi-versions, mainly "family resemblance" and "hypertextuality." But first let us have another look at the familiar concept of adaptation vis-à-vis multiple versions.

I   Versions

Cinematic adaptation and successive cinematic versions of the same source (literary, lyric or mythic) are intersecting, but not identical, fields of study. Any cinematic text which is a recoding of one system of signification into another (literary into filmic systems, for example) is perforce an *adaptation*. If this act repeats itself and the source generates *multiple versions*, then the same filmic text may wear both caps simultaneously, constituting both an adaptation and a cinematic version. The cardinal theoretical question that preoccupies adaptation studies is that of cinematic language, its specific codes and signifiers. This is a question which focuses on the passage from one system of signification to another, from a verbal system to a cinematic one.[6] Theories of cinematic versions, on the other hand, shift the focus and concentrate on poetic and cultural norms within the same system (cinema) over the course of its history.[7] Consequently, the phenomenon of cinematic adaptation demands a comparison between a source and its cinematic concretization (a one-to-one correspondence), while that of cinematic versions inspired by the same source invites a comparative analysis of source and its numerous concretizations as well as a comparison between and among the versions themselves.

Thus, cinematic versions, as members of the same group or category (versions of "X") may behave according to Wittgenstein's principle of *family resemblance*. Wittgenstein (1958) points out that while members of a family resemble one another in various ways, there need to be no single collection of properties shared by everyone in the family.[8] Implementation of this principle with respect to versions, symbolically denoted by characters "A" to "E" and comprising components "a" to "h", will produce the following scheme: [9]

Version A may include components a, b, c, d.
Version B may include components b, c, d, e.
Version C may include components c, d, e, f.
Version D may include components d, e, f, g.
Version E may include components e, f, g, h, i.

Obviously, the *a priori* identification of constant elements can never be exhaustive enough. However, *a posteriori*, a core of element(s) shared by all versions is discernible and analytically significant. For an illuminating illustration of such sub-groups, I will turn to Hofstadter's discussion of the meta-font problematic.

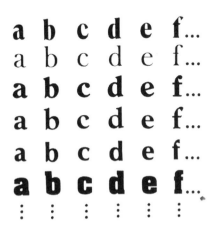

Table 1: "The question amounts to asking how do you see a *variable* where there is actually a *constant*?"(Hofstadter 1985b [1982]: 251).

Cinematic versions stand one vis-à-vis the other like the letters in the chart above set in different fonts. Each group, or rather each sub-group, of versions (e.g., the *Carmen* group) has common features that can be identified only *a posteriori*. As the different fonts will testify, there is clearly also a dynamic of variation among members of the group. This, however, accounts for the vertical dimension only. As Hofstadter claims, any description of the members of a group (or those of a category) requires the simultaneous treatment of both the vertical and the horizontal dimensions of the phenomenon in question; "Vertical – what do all the items in any column have in common? Horizontal – what do all the items in any row have in common?" (Hofstadter, 1985b [1982]: 283).

If all the characters "a" in the chart stand for versions of *Carmen*, for example, the other character groups stand for other sub-groups such as versions of *Anna Karenina* or *Jeanne d'Arc*. Interestingly, versions that belong to different sub-groups might display common aesthetic and/or cultural features along the horizontal dimension. They are written, as it were, in the same font. By analogy, in the denouements of both CARMEN (1915) and JEANNE D'ARC (1916) by DeMille, the death scenes closing both films bear the clear fingerprints of their common *auteur*.

II   Intertextual Sources

Official and nonofficial sources provide *Carmen* with its genetic code, one that will be imprinted on the versions to follow.[10] I refer here not only to Mérimée's story and Bizet's opera, but also to the influences of cultural and musical clichés and stereotypes on the concept of Carmen in popular culture.

The story of *Carmen* has two official sources: Prosper Mérimée's novella of 1845 and Georges Bizet's opera of 1875. But according to Mérimée, the story itself was an *"objet trouvé"*. Napoleon the Third married a Spaniard, Eugenie de Montijo, whose mother was a close friend of Mérimée. It was apparently the Countess of Montijo, the mother of the Empress, who first told the story of Carmen to Mérimée, a habitué of the Imperial Court (in Furman, 1998).

On a romantic quest in Andalusia to discover the location of the ancient battlefield of Munda, Mérimée's narrator accidentally meets Don José, a former officer and wanted criminal, and prevents his being turned over to the authorities. He also meets the beautiful Carmen, on the banks of the Guadalquivir River. She promises to read him his fortune, when they are surprised by the arrival of Don José. The third part of the novella is structured as a confession of Carmen's murder by Don José, in which the dreadful love story of Carmen and Don

José is recounted. The novella concludes with an epilogue in the form of a didactic account of gypsy life, language and habits.

The opera *Carmen* had its premiere in Paris on March 3, 1895. Bizet composed the music, Henri Meilhac and Ludovic Halévy wrote the libretto.[11] Like Mérimée's story, Bizet's opera is divided into four parts (acts/chapters) although its structure is, in other respects, entirely different. The first act brings in Micaëla, looking for Don José, and then Carmen together with Don José and Zuniga, thus creating the two triangles of the relationship: Carmen/Don José /Zuniga (later Escamillo) and Don José/Carmen/Micaëla. The second act, which takes place in Lillas Pastia's tavern, focuses on the characterization of the leading figures. While developing the relationship between Carmen and Don José, it does not neglect Zuniga, whom Don José kills. As a result he is forced to join the gypsy smugglers. The third act, located in the mountain pass, is the grand hour of the triangles: Micaëla pursues Don José who loves Carmen, while Escamillo, a toreador, pursues Carmen, who no longer loves Don José. In the fourth and last act, in a square in Seville, Escamillo arrives at the arena with Carmen beside him. Don José follows Carmen, and while the crowd applauds Escamillo, Don José murders her.[12]

Unofficial sources have also played a significant role in the reception space of the text. It might even be argued that what characterizes *Carmen* as an opera are its imperfections in the sense that it is a collage of various themes that had already been used successfully elsewhere.[13]

The overture to *Carmen* presents us with a few distinctive motifs: the colorful sounds of the Spanish carnival and the excitement of the impending bullfight. This highly spirited music is interrupted for a while by the steady beat of the world-famous Toreador Song, glowing in its orchestral version, after which the orchestra sounds the terrifying Fate motif and the curtain rises. As Biancoli and Bayer note, the first melodic line of the overture, which reappears in the excitement of Act IV, is a Spanish theme (Biancoli and Bayer, 1953: 61-2). In addition, the "[…] Fate motif – that five-note phrase with the augmented second that sums up, with its somber inevitability, the entire tragedy" (Biancoli, 1953: 77) – also bears the traces of another work of art and was actually the main reason for Bizet's being accused of imitating Wagner (Golea, ibid.: 2).

The *Habañera* aria that marks Carmen's entrance in Act I is based, according to Donington (1978), on an authentically Spanish theme, *El-Alregito*, "a tune which Bizet borrowed – seemingly taking it for a folk tune, though it is actually by the Spanish-American composer Yradier" (Donington, ibid.: 173).[14] Susan McClary observes that : "… the *Habañera* was lifted expressly from the Parisian cabaret scene." (1997: 123). Pushkin's "Les Bohemiens" was apparently the inspiration for Carmen's scorching challenge to the authorities in Act I (Biancolli, 1953: 75), while the *seguidilla* that Carmen dances for Don José is Bizet's own music, with flamenco rhythms and intervals. But most significant of all is the "sustained exotic atmosphere – *Spanish in imagination* [...] to which the chromatic intervals and the piquant rhythms contribute" (Donington, 1978: 173, emphasis added). This "Spanishness" is mediated through a ready-made, second-degree representation of Spain, expressed via the gypsy and toreador figures, as well as through the free motives of the *Habañera* and the Toreador Song – now almost a part of our folk music" (ibid.).

In his essay, "*Casablanca*, Cult Movies and Intertextual Collage" (1986 [1984]), Umberto Eco asserts that a work of art gains cult status if its separate parts can be isolated. Only an imperfect work of art, he adds, may be segmented and still gain meaning. The parts which tend to be candidates for such segmentation have the special charm of the already known, the familiar (ibid.). It is within this context I am considering *Carmen*'s popularity and the exceptional number of cinematic versions that have been made in its wake. It is not only the dramatic positioning that endows *Carmen* with its fatal attraction; it is also the "dangerous" desire encapsulated in the figure of the gypsy woman and her songs and the seductive charms of the déjà vu.

III   Variability

The reading of various cinematic versions seeks, on the one hand, to describe the uniqueness of each version and, on the other, to discover what is common to them all. Whether it is the novella, the opera, some combination of the two or a previous cinematic version, the presence of the source(s) as a manifest or latent influence is part of the dynamic which defines the *Carmen* group. Hence, two factors participate in this dynamic: the attitude of the particular version towards *Carmen* as a cultural object and the spectator's intertextual knowledge.

A   Representation and Transformation of the Sources

A version may represent the events, characters and structure of the source as a whole, or represent these components selectively. It may transform the source at various levels, partially or globally; Raoul Walsh's silent version (1927) for example, suggests an entirely different narrative structure than his sources to the extent that he focuses on Carmen's relationship with Escamillo, the toreador. Escamillo appears quite early on, and Carmen's main interest consists in arousing his love. Within the framework of this plot, Don José is a rather minor figure who propels the story to its tragic end, without much encouragement on Carmen's part. Christian-Jaque's World War II production (1943-45), on the other hand, emphasizes the idea of mutual assistance in the face of the enemy, and involves changes mainly at secondary levels of the narrative.[15] While Otto Preminger's version (1954) suggests a global transformation of location, time and characters.

What differentiates the relation of these three versions towards the *Carmen* sources is the level of transformation: "cardinal functions" and "indexes" (Barthes's terminology, 1977 [1966]) of the narrative, affecting the whole narrative structure, have been added to Walsh's and Christian-Jaque's versions, whereas "catalysts" and "informators" (ibid.) have transformed Preminger's version.[16]

The question of the transformation of the sources should also take into account the state of the element(s) involved – interpolations and extrapolations. Thus, a version may modify the source with respect to its order, characterization, structure or hierarchy of dominance of components. It may omit certain elements or extrapolate new ones from existing elements. Godard's version is an example of extrapolations and interpolations where the story of the bank robbery, the story of the self-institutionalized Uncle Jean, the film production and the love triangle all become fragmented plot-lines intersecting one another. Francesco Rosi's CARMEN (1984) is another example: by using the rhetorical device of flashback, he changes the order of reception, and hence of signification, of some cardinal narrative functions. Since Mérimée himself used this technique, Rosi's functional shift may be seen to interpolate between this source and Rosi's manifest source – Bizet's opera. (For Rosi's CARMEN see ill. I & VIII b)

B   Relation to the Model

According to Barbara Hernstein Smith, "The form and features of any 'version' of a narrative will be a function of, among other things, the particular motives that elicited it and the particular interests and functions it was designed to serve" (Hernstein Smith, 1980: 222). The concept of "Carmen," or the model perceived by the versions, may introduce adaptations of the primary sources, i.e., Mérimée and Bizet. Their original concepts may be challenged, however, by a new approach, or even rejected and replaced by an entirely new concept of "Carmen."

In addition to interpolations, extrapolations are involved in versions like those of Chaplin, A BURLESQUE ON CARMEN (1916), or Amadori, CARMEN (1943). These versions challenge *Carmen*'s pre-texts, locating them within the diegetic world of the text as a second-degree reality. In Chaplin's A BURLESQUE ON CARMEN, three pre-texts are manipulated – Mérimée's novella, Bizet's opera, and DeMille's film. Chaplin transforms *Carmen* into a parody, conflating two triangles: Carmen/the toreador/Don José and Preckita/the Bully/the Tramp.

While quoting visually from DeMille, Chaplin writes his own interpretation over DeMille's tableau (like a palimpsest). This is evident in a few scenes as, for example, towards the end of the film, Chaplin rehearses the concluding scene of DeMille's CARMEN. Don José seizes his knife and chases after the fleeing Carmen. He kills her and kisses her as the title appears with the words, "Oh, well, two can die as well as one." He then thrusts the knife into his side and falls on Carmen's body. Soon after this both Carmen and Don José rise to their feet, smiling, and Chaplin shows Carmen that the knife is only a stage prop.

Luis César Amadori's version locates *Carmen* as an opera performance within the diegetic world of the film, turning it into a *Bildungsroman*. Amadori's heroine rejects the advances of the young man who works with her. In a comedy of errors, she becomes involved in the opera production of *Carmen* where she improvises, sending the plot totally out of control. In the scene where Don José is supposed to kill her, she faints, breaks her leg, and eventually finds herself behind the scenes. There she confesses that her attraction to the Carmen figure has waned. Eventually, she happily returns the love of her suitor.

The textual levels of Chaplin's and Amadori's films hide another text whose presence is persistently echoed throughout the film. An ideal reading of these versions means oscillating among the present text (Chaplin's or Amadori's), the primary sources (Mérimée, Bizet) and previous cinematic versions.

C   Relative Degree of Entropy: Overcoding/Undercoding

The relative entropy of a text indicates the degree of disorientation created in a specific version. As Ziva Ben-Porat states: "Maximum entropy occurs only in the absence of all content-bearing units, mutual patterning functions and laws of combination. Minimum entropy occurs when the number of elements to be combined is very small, and the text allows only one possible manner of combination" (1985: 171, my translation). Thus, the potential intertextual relations between a source and its versions are governed, first by the representational mode of the source (manifest or latent, in the title, characters' names, cardinal events, etc.); and, secondly, by the addressee's previous knowledge.

Carlos Saura's CARMEN (1983) involves two levels of reality: the story of the production and the concept of "Carmen" arising from primary sources, as presented in the ballet. In this version, the events selected for the ballet function on both levels of reality. Thus, the brawl between Carmen and Manuelita in the tobacco factory of the ballet allows the two women to express their professional rivalry on the production level. The erotic tension between Carmen and Don José (in the ballet) parallels the tension between Antonio and his chosen Carmen/dancer. The scene in which Escamillo courts Carmen to Don José's jealous reaction involves both levels of reality, blurring the borders between the two, while the last scene, in which Don José/Antonio murders Carmen/Carmen, re-inforces this ambiguity. Is this the resolution of Carmen and Antonio's story as well or does it only follow the original story in the embedded fiction?

Jean-Luc Godard, in his version, uses the entropy produced by the parallel plot-lines in order to expose and challenge the signification of Carmen's tale in Western culture. During the opening sequence, while the titles are running, one can hear Carmen's voice saying that the title should be *Before the Name, Before Language*. And in brackets one sees *Children Playing Carmen*. The opening scene can be read as follows: Since the name "Carmen" already embodies the culture of Mérimée, Bizet and all previous cinematic versions, Godard would like to examine the question of what preceded this. Thus, the film presents fragments of stories, characters, music (the fragment of a Beethoven quartet) and paintings (with emphasis on Van Gogh's yellow) taken out of their cultural context. Contrary to the tradition that has been established since Mérimée, in Godard's film it is Carmen who relates to culture, while the men (Uncle Jean, Joseph) relate to the primordial world that operates outside culture.

Peter Brook's *The Tragedy of Carmen* (1984), first produced on stage in London with three alternative casts appearing in rotation, can be used here as an example for overcoding. The film is composed of three successive versions of the play in which the *mise-en-scène* and editing are identical, but each has a different cast. The game involving the successive modifications of an actor's physiognomy, movements and vocal qualities emphasizes the work behind the text, while simultaneously exposing the formal principle behind the relativity of each version: variability ad infinitum.

Like Godard and Saura, Brook's interest lies not in challenging the course of the story – none of them believes in the ultimate story – but in the process of conceptualization. By presenting a selective narrative skeleton with extrapolations, all three increase the degree of entropy and cause the spectator to contemplate the meaning of the story at the end of the 20th century.

IV Carmen's Chain

The process of reading and comparing selected versions produces a palimpsest dialogue between a later text (*a hypertext*) and an earlier text (*a hypotext*), an activity defined by Gérard Genette as a *hypertextual relationship* (1982). In the hypertextual chain of *Carmen*, two parallel processes of transformation appear and not necessarily in a diachronic order: (1) Extrapolation/Erosion and (2) Originality/Repetition.

I   Extrapolation/Erosion

Versions like those of DeMille, Walsh or Rosi aim to be faithful to the model in their concretized reconstructions. In versions like those of Amadori, Saura or Godard it is enough to represent the narrative structure only partially. Despite the fact that extrapolation is causally related to a high degree of entropy, the effect is partly neutralized because of the canonic status of the myth in culture.

2   Originality/Repetition

From a traditional text that aspires to the presentation of a perfect reconstruction via interpolated versions which emphasize originality and suggest the subjective vision of the concept of "Carmen," the progressive treatment of the versions culminates in a multi-diegetic text which creates a meta-discourse through an open dialogue on originality and repetition.

As the reading of the *Carmen* group shows, hypertextual relationships between "multi-versions" involve: (a) a derivative relationship between a source and its cinematic version, wherein the hypotext can be either the common source or a previous version or versions; (b) relations between the source and each one of its "multi-versions," as well as the cumulative effect of the successive chain of versions; and (c) potential relations among the versions themselves. However, the concretization of a potential link between a given version and previous version or source is brought about by the viewer and belongs to his/her reception space.[17]

In the process of rewriting the Carmen story, two types of repetition can be discerned, and Genette's distinction can be used here as a starting point. According to Genette (ibid.) the operative mechanism underlying a hypertext like Virgil's *Aeneid* or Joyce's *Ulysses* is generative, that is, a transformation of the hypotexts of Homer. But the two texts engage in different kinds of transformation. Joyce's *Ulysses* is a "direct transformation" that includes substitute components: Joyce tells the story of Ulysses in a style that differs from that of Homer. Virgil's *Aeneid,* on the other hand, is a "complicated and less direct transformation," or an "imitation." Virgil tells a different story *in the style* of Homer.[18] Genette's model, however, does not take into consideration different cultural reactions to the same hypotext. His model ignores, for example, the fact that hypertexts like those of Preminger or Godard have differing affinities to Mérimée's and Bizet's hypotexts. In order to overcome this deficiency, I will employ Ben-Porat's distinction between metaphorical and metonymical allusion, and her treatment of their varying effects (1976). According to Ben-Porat, a *metaphorical* allusion has the effect of reinforcing the connection between the alluding and the alluded-to text, while a *metonymical* allusion has the effect of distancing the two texts from each other. A synthesis between Ben-Porat's principle of metaphorical and metonymical allusion, on the one hand, and Genette's distinction between direct transformation and imitation, on the other, will enable us to produce a more accurate classification of versions and their cultural functions.

I.   Imitation   II.   Direct Transformation

            IIa. metaphorical   IIb. metonymical
                  transformation   transformation
                  (Preminger's version)   (Godard's version)

Fig. 2: Genette's Model (Revised)

The various cinematic versions of *Carmen* seem to shift the focus from a generative relationship between one text and its precursor to variability as a formal and cultural principle. However, the chain of *Carmen*, like all other chains, is not preordained. To understand it fully, one must identify not only its sources but also its components, both manifest and latent. Constancy and variability are the crux of the matter. Hypertextuality, as the *a posteriori* construction of a given interrelated corpus, allows the observation of features which are normally hidden or undetected in any given single version.

Within the dynamic of repetition and variation in the *Carmen* corpus, we can identify Carmen's first aria, the *Habañera*, as a constant element in the inventory examined, repeating itself again and again in the hypertexts. However, I will argue, Carmen's voice has been consistently muted by the cinematic institution. Is it possible that it is precisely this silencing that will enable us to understand the enormous popularity of the story?

Notes

1. For a discussion of the musical adaptation in *Carmen Jones* see Jeremy Tambling (1987).
2. Whose relations with her are reminiscent of Humbert Humbert's relations with Lolita (Vladimir Nabokov, 1955).
3. Among the non-filmic adaptations of *Carmen* it is worth mentioning Pablo Picasso's 38 engravings, published with the 1949 edition of *Carmen* (Paris, 1949), Roland Petite's ballet (French TV3 production, 1980), the computer game series *Carmen San Diego* (1991, USA), a short video by Laurie Anderson (1992, USA) and *Car-Man*, a ballet by Mathew Bourne (2001, UK).
4. *Carmen* is the most frequently filmed of all operas (see Jennifer Batchelor, 1984).

5.   The sources are not identical and list different items. According to electronic sources the data are even higher (IMDb, Cinemania, and BFI index, 2001). According to the Carmen Project now underway at the University of Newcastle upon Tyne, UK, there are no less than 77 versions. Their listing also includes various opera recordings (URL: http: //www.ncl.ac.uk/crif/carlist).

6.   Among the rich bibliographies on filmic adaptations, I would like to mention here especially: Jury Tynianov (1981 [1927]), Christian Metz (1974, 1979), Deborah Cartmeli & Imelda Whelehan (1999), Robert Stam (2000) and James Naremore (2000).

7.   See also on remake and remaking the discussion by Daniel Protopopoff & Michel Serceau (1989), Thomas M. Leitch, (1990), Constantine Vervis (1997), Andrew Horton & Stuart Y. McDougal (eds.), (1998). On multi-versions see Anat Zanger (1993, 2001) and multi-versions in Shakespeare see Peter Donaldson (1996).

8.   Thus, a category such as "game," for example, like that of family members, will include items that are similar to one another in a wide variety of ways, but share no single, well-defined collection of common properties.

9.   My use of *family resemblance* here is inspired by Claude Bremond's implementation of Wittgenstein's theory in Claude Bremond (1985).

10. This subject will be examined in the next two chapters from both a textual and a cultural point of view.

11. Tchaikovsky, who heard the opera in Paris the following year, prophesied that "in ten years it will become the most popular opera in the world," and, indeed, it did (in Lockspeiser, 1967-8: 11).

12. The plot summary, like any reading, is already an interpretative act, and since there are a number of possible readings of *Carmen*, it is only to be expected that there should be no consensus regarding the synopsis either. See also Chapter 4.

13. Following Eco's definition of a "cult movie" (1986).

14. Biancolli adds that Bizet's acknowledgment to Yradier's publishers in the first edition of *Carmen* testifies to the fact that he borrowed one number, a banal ballad, *El Areglito*, for Carmen's entrance (in Biancolli [ed.] 1953: 76).

15. As Barthes (1974 [1970]) has pointed out, the cultural code will always betray the period of a text's production.

16. On the application of Roland Barthes "The Structural Analysis of Narratives" to film, see Anat Zanger (1993) and Brian McFarlane (1996). Other parameters, such as changes in the cultural setting of the film, as suggested by Robert Eberwein in Horton & McDougal (1998: 28-30), intersect with mine.

17. This activity has already been termed "intertextuality" in its broader sense (see Kristeva 1969, Barthes 1974 [(1970)] and, more specifically, "rhetorical transtextuality" (see Genette, 1982 and Eco, 1988 [1984]). According to Ziva Ben-Porat (1990) transtextuality, in its wider sense, is a necessary procedure for understanding and identification. "Rhetorical transtextuality," on the other hand, is an optional activity which functions as part of the text's poetics. For discussion on adaptation as transtextual activity see in Anat Zanger (1993, 2001) and Robert Stam (2000).

18. Genette exemplifies the differences between these two kinds of text through the schematic opposition of "saying the same thing differently" ("*dire la même chose autrement*") (Joyce), versus "saying a different thing in a similar manner" ("*dire autre chose semblablement*") (Virgil) (ibid.: 13). Genette distinguishes between ludicrous, satiric and serious modes of hypertextuality, of which the most complicated is the

serious transformation – which he calls a "transposition." This latter type of transformation, and its weight within a chain of transformations, constitutes the focus of my interest in the present study.

Chapter 3
Muted Voices

Robert Townsend's MTV *Carmen: A Hip Hopera* (2001), can be used here as an example of palimpsestic writing, in which Townsend has transformed the high-brow operatic music and libretto into an updated, hip-hop musical production.[1] In one of the more significant sequences in this version – the seduction scene – Beyoncé Knowles, as Carmen, sings to Hill the policeman (= Don José). Along with the hip-hop beat, familiar musical phrases are repeated several times. Interposed in the musical score and woven into the new version, they function as familiar signposts of an impending tragedy. These phrases, and especially a few familiar phrases from the *Habañera*, are identifiable as Bizet's music. In order to maintain the spectators' pleasure, however, Townsend has adopted the coarse hip-hop style only partially and refrains from giving Carmen's credo its full performance.

Act I of *Carmen*, the opera, is structured so as to make the *Habañera* its main theme. This occurs at the moment when Don José kneels to pick up the flower (the glove, as it were)[2] cast at him by Carmen, thus declaring the central, anticipated conflict of the plot.[3] The *Habañera*, with its metaphor of rebellious love, condenses the central problematic of the tale, that of Carmen's social transgression.[4] In this sense the *Habañera*, from DeMille (1915) to Aranda (2003), is also present in versions that use Mérimée as their main source. It provides one of the "main knobs" (to use Hofstadter's term, 1985a [1982]), through which we can follow the same element in the different versions, that is, the varying "twists" of this core element of *Carmen*, and explain its secret charm.

I   *Olympia*

In order to exemplify the game between constant and variable while introducing the cultural dimension of repetitions, I will turn first to the famous painting *Olympia* and its chain of variations. Notably, Manet's *Olympia* (1865) was inspired by Titian's *The Venus of Urbino* (1538), which was in turn inspired by Giorgione's *The Sleeping Venus* (1509-10), and then functioned as a source of inspiration for numerous visual rewritings over the course of the 20th century.

Culture, so it seems, had replaced the original "source" of inspiration with a derivative model, itself functioning as a new "source." Manet's text, born as a rewriting of previous paintings, has in itself come to constitute a point of reference in a long cultural and aesthetic dialogue featuring Giorgione (1509-10), Titian (1530), Manet (1865), Picasso (*Parody of Manet Olympia*, 1901), Vallotton (*The Black & The White*, 1913), Villon (*Manet, Olympia*, 1926), Magritte (*Olympia*, 1947), Erro (United States, 1983), Kushner (*Olympia – Robert and José*, 1983), Rutault (*Michel Delluc-10 Avril, 1983*), Morimura (*Olympia*, 1988) and Katarzyna Kozyra (*Olympia*, 1996) to mention some of the most significant links. (For Manet's *Olympia* see ill. IV a)

It becomes apparent that some rewritings of *Olympia* make their relations to the model manifest through their titles (Picasso, Villon, Kushner), but not all of them do so. The first artist to mask Venus' genealogy by changing the title was none other than Manet himself and, as we shall see, this was not accidental. The appeal of *Olympia* lies in its bitter rejection of the ideological consensus, and in its querulousness, as well as in its inconsistency (Wollen, 1980). *Olympia* represents an imaginary spectatorship of domination, as if the viewer, by means of his/her gaze, were able to achieve dominance over the female figure of Olympia. But unlike *The Venus of Urbino* and other traditional texts which represent the woman as a spectacle, *Olympia* simultaneously signals obedience and disobedience (See also Foucault (2004 [1971]),Clark, 1980, Wollen, 1980). Through its contradictory codes of perception (line, lighting, color), and through the positioning of the figure of Olympia (her direct look, her powerful hand position, the location of the cat beside her), the painting reflects both compliance and its negation, exhibiting and exposing a dialectic that refuses to collaborate with the existing ideological configuration[5]. Wollen's and, later, Bernheimer's interpretations (Bernheimer, 1989) seek to explain the ambiguities that constitute the puzzling representation of *Olympia*, suggesting that *Olympia* is, in Wollen's words, "[a] picture which is not about 'Woman' but the production of woman as a fetish in a particular conjunction of capitalism and patriarchy" (1980: 23). As observed by Mieke Bal (1993) *Olympia* "[...] suggests that the regime in which it functions does not allow a communicative functioning of vision. It simultaneously displays and refuses that difficulty, and remains in the negativity that results" (ibid.: 392). In this sense, *Olympia* might be perceived as depicting the classical mode of representation pointing towards its own functioning. Paradoxically, only when a viewer identifies the place of the subject do the codes which led her/him to occupy this place become visible to her/him.

Olympia apparently crosses the boundaries between the sacred and the profane – hence, its followers must attempt to reconstitute these boundaries once again. *Olympia* seems to be the most subversive text of all, at least from our limited perspective in the early twenty-first century. If *Madame Bovary,* "one of the founding texts of modernism" (Huyssen 1986: 44) posits the woman-reader and the man-writer in a set of oppositions, Manet's *Olympia* reshuffles the alignment. Oppositions such as active/passive, subjective/objective, and rational/emotional (see Huyssen, ibid.: 45), cannot possibly be related to one sex or another, since they are all given in the dialectical tension of contradictory worlds.

II   Re-Significations

Looking at the "re-significations" of Manet's *Olympia* over the centuries, it is possible to isolate three components, three knobs if we like, that can be twisted over and over: (a) The relations between Olympia and the male figure (who is only symbolically present in Manet's painting as the owner of the gaze); (b) The relations between Olympia and her handmaid; (c) The relations between whites and blacks. Gender, class and racial domination are all variables in the rewriting of *Olympia*, while the later works all seem to seek a stand vis-à-vis the riddle that Manet had articulated.[6]

The desire to have the already known experience repeated is accompanied by the presentiment that it never will be. "Repetition and difference have firstly to be understood in their relationship to desire, pleasure and *jouissance*, i.e., as modalities of the process of the subject," observes Steve Neale (1980: 48). The subject-viewer oscillates between the initial experience of pleasure, the traces left by this experience, and future attempts to repeat it. Pleasure is located in the moment of homeostasis between tension and release, that is, when difference and repetition are in equilibrium. *Jouissance*, in contrast, relates to the freezing of the moment of the annihilation of tension, that is, when differences and repetition are not satisfactorily balanced (see also Roland Barthes, 1977, and Willemen, 1975, cited in Neale 1980: 48). The reception space of the version is thus constituted by the dialectical movement of desire, whose precondition is that the spectators identify the "new" text as a repetition. In Barthes's own words:

> Text of pleasure: the text that contents, fills, grants euphoria; the text that comes from culture and does not break with it, is linked to a comfortable practice of reading. Text of bliss [*jouissance*]: the text that imposes a state of loss, the text that discomforts (perhaps to the point of boredom), unsettles the reader's historical, cultural, psychological assumptions, the consistency of his tastes, values, memories, brings to crisis his relation with language (1975 [1973]: 14).

In this sense, Giorgione's painting, by metaphorically transforming Titian's painting, is an ultimate actualization of pleasure. Manet's *Olympia*, on the other hand, by refusing to position the figure of the woman within the conventions of "to-be-looked-at-ness" brings into crisis the very experience of spectatorship and produces a state of loss: the viewer finds that traditional pleasure has been destroyed and *jouissance* suggested instead. Manet's metonymic transformation challenged the traditional mode of representing female sexuality, and the versions that followed aimed to correct it by repeating it. As suggested in the introductory chapter, serial repetitions turn the repetitive object (figure, painting or story) into a stereotyped fetish, by means of concealment and denial. In this way, cultural institutions domesticate the chosen object by turning it into one that evokes pleasure.

III   *Carmen*'s Transgression

Since the 18th century, as Michel Foucault has observed (1976), sexual discourse is pronounced not outside the power foci but within its own sites. In order for sexuality to be governed, it has to be examined and to develop procedures of discourse. Thus, Carmen may express her sexual freedom in the opera and cinema – but before the curtain falls, *sexual order must be restored*. Patriarchal society uses Carmen's "desire for desire," asserted in her first aria and expressed in her relations with Don José, as a "pocket of resistance." It is ideologically embraced, conditionally, and then rejected in the denouement with the kiss of death.

Mérimée's Carmen is represented only through the eyes of men, two to be exact: the narrator and Don José. The former describes her as a "sorceress," "the devil's daughter," and says that "hers was a wild and savage beauty," citing a Spanish proverb that describes gypsy eyes as "wolf eyes" (1963 [1845]: 29, 30). Don José, for his part, compares her to a filly, speaks of her "diabolic smile" and "crocodile laughter," to mention only a few of his characterizations (ibid.: 58). A flashback further conveys the love story of Carmen and Don José in which she employs witchcraft to seduce him. She has, after all, struck out at masculine honor and the rule of law by her seductive wiles and moral deficiency.

In the opera, on the other hand, Carmen is obviously her own spokeswoman, allowed to sing her own song. But, we may ask: "Who listens to the words in an opera?" Words in an opera, according to Catherine Clément (1989 [1986]), "are seldom understood. The music makes one forget the plot." In the case of *Carmen*, this involves the oppression and murder of a woman intent on following her own desires. The plot and words are not innocent. On the contrary, beyond the captivating music "lines are being woven, tying up the characters and leading them to death for transgression – of familial and political roles."(ibid.: 9-10).

Contemporary interpretations read the structure of the opera as a systematic network of oppositions in which Carmen and Don José are located in polar positions. In Dominique Maingeneau's analysis (1984) *Carmen* is a drama of conflict and tension between locations – village, town and mountains – that work around the oppositions of order and disorder. According to Clément, lighting also has its own code of oppositions in the symbolism of the opera: "By day Carmen is in prison; by night she is the winner and Don José the deserter for her sake. By night she is in command; in the brilliant sun of bullfights she dies." (1989 [1986]: 51-2). The social and moral orders, with their attendant violence, represented through the symbolism of locations and lighting, are deeply linked to the language of love in the opera. To quote Nelly Furman:

> Whether we see José as victim or Carmen as martyr, we are forever caught in the mirror image of a master/slave relationship, where the two main characters are reflections of each other. In the *corrida* of passionate love, both Carmen and José occupy in turn the position of bullfighter and bull (1988: 172).

IV Filming the *Habañera*

Carmen's social transgressions are inscribed in all parts of the opera but nowhere more succinctly than in the *Habañera*. In a vein similar to that of *Olympia*, they are inscribed with a feminine declaration of simultaneous obedience and disobedience:

> *L'amour est un oiseau rebelle* (Love is a rebellious bird)
> *Que nul ne peut apprivoiser,* (That nobody can tame,)
> *Et c'est bien en vain qu'on l'appelle* (And it's all in vain to call it)
> *S'il lui convient de refuser.* (If it chooses to refuse.)

Carmen will repeat these lines later on, and she will add:

> *Si tu ne m'aimes pas, je t'aime* (Though you don't love me, I love you)
> *Si je t'aime, prends garde à toi.* (And if I love you, then beware.)[7]

It is not only the words that introduce Carmen that have an "impure," indirect, seductive quality. It is the music as well. As Susan McClary (1989) observes in her foreword to Clément's *Opera or the Undoing of Women*, the music cues us on how to regard Carmen:

> Carmen makes her first appearance with the slippery descent of her *"Habañera"*, and it is her harmonic promiscuity – which threatens to undermine Don José's drive for

> absolute tonal closure at the conclusion of the opera – that finally renders her death *musically* necessary (McClary, 1989: xiii).

She is definitely a vamp, perhaps even a tramp, and no good can possibly come of her. "The tonal cards are stacked against Carmen from the outset" (ibid.: xiv).

The cinematic transformations of *Carmen* are intriguing in the ways in which the rhetorical devices are employed in the rewriting of the libretto, the adaptation of the music and the performative gestures of the actors' bodies. In the wake of Clément's observation that the pleasure of listening to music often obstructs our ability to listen to the words and absorb their meaning, we may ask: how does this work in the cinematic rewriting? Does the cinematic institution foreground the words and the plot, making them plainly visible to all while remaining, at the same time, outside of the pleasure code of the opera? Does the cinematic institution use its own machinery of visual pleasure in the process of retelling Carmen's story? The versions discussed here are selected links in a continuous process of re-reading by filmmakers and spectators, all of whom take part in a reception space in which *Carmen* is simultaneously appropriated and silenced.

Silent *Carmen*

Early cinema presentations were based on two elements: a mechanical moving image and a live instrumental, often orchestral, accompaniment, though not actual recordings of the opera. As for the absence of the voice itself, Mary Ann Doane observes (1986 [1980]):

> The absent voice reemerges in gestures and the contortions of the face – it is spread over the body of the actor. The uncanny effect of the silent film in the era of sound is in part linked to the *separation*, by means of intertitles, of an actor's speech from the image of his/ her body (ibid.: 335, emphasis added).

In versions like those of DeMille (1915), Chaplin (1916), Lubitsch (1918), Feyder (1926) and Walsh (1927), the subtitles on the screen provide emotional cues to follow as well as information needed to develop the plot. None of them, however, gives Carmen's *Habañera* a full recital. The "separation" in these versions is between word and body as well as between word and music. In DeMille's version, for example (I refer to the restored version of 1996), in which Carmen was performed by the famous diva, Geraldine Farrar, accompanied by live music at the Boston Symphony Hall, the *Habañera* was divided into five segments, but never performed in its entirety.[8] A few phrases from the aria are heard – twice with the words and three times without them – but the aria is never heard in sync with the visuals. The *Habañera* functions as background music in order to create the right atmosphere for the temptation of Don José. In a homage to Geraldine Farrar two of Carmen's important arias are heard in full right after the credits, but the *Habañera* is heard again only in part, while the visuals depict newspaper headlines and information about the performance and Farrar's career, competing with the *Habañera* and, in fact, "drowning out" Carmen's words.

Despite the narrative transformations of DeMille's version, Chaplin's *A Burlesque on Carmen,* by omitting altogether any reference to the operatic music, and especially the *Habañera,* misses the opportunity of dealing with Carmen's credo.[9] The selective use of Carmen's voice and the segmentation/erosion of the *Habañera* in both DeMille's and Chaplin's films have a special meaning in the viewing process that characterized the silent era. The use of subtitles, as observed by Neale (1985), Doane (1986), Chion (1999) and others, meant a separation between actor, title and spectator. This process transmits the enunciation level of dialogue and libretto from the actor to the spectator. As Steve Neale remarks: "In the absence of the recording of the actor's voice, a voice was provided by each spectator individually" (1985: 94).[10]

Muted *Carmen*

Talkies seem to have multiple possibilities for recording the music, translating the libretto via subtitles and presenting it along with Carmen's gestures on the visual channel of the movie. With the standardization of sound, "… sounds and images are homogenized, unified, bound together across the 'body' of a single text, a single 'space' of meaning and perception" (Neale, ibid.: 99). A number of talking versions filmed the operatic text and music, without complementary subtitles; others transformed the music and the libretto.

Female director Lotte Reiniger's (1933) animated shadow version of *Carmen* was accompanied by musical themes from the opera, especially those from the overture, the *Habañera* and the Toreador Song. In this exceptional version Carmen charms the bull with a flower and wins the toreador. The operatic text, however, was transformed into music without words. Luis César Amadori's version (1943) ends with the same denouement: Carmen remains alive, but like Chaplin's version (1916), his *Carmen* is only a show within a show. In this version, Carmen sings the *Habañera,* on stage and for the first time in her life in front of a full house, but her credo is questioned and deconstructed both by the amateur who performs the aria and by the denouement, where the heroine happily returns her suitor's love. Otto Preminger's *Carmen Jones* (1954) transfers the plot to the United States of the 1950s and Oscar Hammerstein's "Dat's Love," "Dere's a Café on the Corner," and "Stan' up to Fight" replace the *Habañera,* the *seguidilla* and the toreador's number (Tambling 1987: 31).

Preminger locates the "Dat's Love" (= *Habañera*) scene in the canteen at the army basis. Joe is having lunch there with Cindy-Lou when Carmen Jones enters with a red flower in her hand. Preminger lets Carmen Jones sing that love is "a baby that grow up wild and don't do what you want him to," using recognizable phrases from the *Habañera*. However, the flower in her hands is replaced by a tray during the number and her gestures gradually blocked through the *mise-en-scène*. Thus, while moving between the long tables in the canteen holding the tray, Carmen's body movements are limited, and when she sits near the table her body is hidden. The "disciplining" of Carmen's body is accompanied by a female chorus who can repeat – now that her body has been sexually controlled – the lines of "Dat's Love" and "If I love you, that the end of you." Through its various filmic channels, *Carmen Jones* both presents and conceals the presence of the *Habañera*. (For Preminger's *Carmen Jones* see ill. III b)

Old and New *Carmen*

Although all technical limitations were removed and the rights to Bizet's opera moved into the public domain, the *postmodernist versions* of the 1980s followed the path of their predecessors. Through the interplay of repetition and innovation, *postmodernist versions*, such as those by Saura, Godard and Brook, suggest a meta-discourse on Carmen in Western culture. However, by keeping the libretto suppressed these versions function as an equivalent of the operatic mechanism that elicits the pleasure only of listening to the music.

Francesco Rosi's *Carmen* (1984) is an acknowledged attempt to visualize Bizet's opera. Rosi generally respects the opera's structure and cast, although he shortens most of the opera's scenes. The soundtrack is a mix of music recorded in the studio months earlier, with dialogue recorded live at the time of shooting.[11] As for the libretto, the mechanism of listening pleasure is not neutralized. It is rather emphasized by the visuals that address themselves to the gaze of the viewer. In the scene introducing Carmen, the heroine is revealed to the audience through the voyeuristic gaze (in Mulvey's sense) of the lieutenant.[12] Thus the pleasure of listening to music is enhanced here by the pleasure of looking at Carmen as she enjoys herself with a few young women by the river, her body wrapped in a wet, almost transparent dress.

Carlos Saura's *Carmen* (1983) is based on and quotes from Mérimée's story while its soundtrack draws on Bizet's music, but it also creates a contemporary musical equivalent of Bizet's music – that of the *bulerias*. Segments of music cited from Bizet's opera function as a pre-text, alerting the initiated spectator familiar with the opera to clues about possible dramatic developments, and also encouraging analogies between the pre-text and what follows. The music from Bizet's opera, however, has another form of presence in Saura's film, through an analogue, namely Paco de Lucia's flamenco music, played on a single instrument, a guitar. Thus, in the film's opening sequence, Carmen's phrases are played on the phonograph and, simultaneously, Paco de Lucia's music is performed. (For Saura's *Carmen* see ill. III a)

In the second sequence, where Carmen rehearses the *Habañera* scene, the duality of sound and musical images blurs the borderline between the two levels of reality as Antonio, the director of the dance troupe, falls in love with his dancer Carmen. Saura directs both Carmen and Antonio performing the *Habañera*: Carmen performs it for Antonio on stage (in the ballet), but it is Antonio who seduces Carmen with the *Habañera* in their lovemaking. Thus, Carmen's phrases, music and gestures, that is, her entire credo, no longer belong only to her.

In *Prénom Carmen* (1983) Jean-Luc Godard uses Mérimée's story of Carmen and Don José in the abstract. Godard also uses themes and figures from Bizet's opera that reinforce the love triangle. Preserving the idea that "*Carmen* wouldn't be *Carmen* without music," Godard rejects Bizet's music and replaces it with Beethoven quartets, performed as part of the cinematic world of the film and its soundtrack.[13] However, in a typical Godardian manner the sole reference to Bizet's music appears as a curious, accidental whistling in the bar. It is – what else? – a tune from the *Habañera*.[14]

In *The Tragedy of Carmen* (1984) Peter Brook rewrites Bizet's music in chamber form, a form reflecting its remote and isolated fictional world. Only cardinal events and notable musical themes have been chosen from the opera. The libretto has been partially changed, partially omitted. Brook refuses to define Carmen in a singular manner; her credo, the *Habañera*, is therefore performed in each of the three successive versions by a different actress: first by a fragile, tortured Carmen (Zehava Gal), then by a naive, romantic one (Helene Delarault), and last by a sensuous temptress (Eva Sauova). The fact that one Carmen after the other is ensnared in the same story underlines the inevitability of her punishment. On the other hand, the words of the *Habañera* are not given a complete performance by any of them.

Another example worth mentioning here is Roland Petit's ballet, a 1980 TV3 production. In Petit's version only a single line is heard. The line, from the *Habañera*, is chanted by a group of seated dancers while Don José (Mikhail Baryshnikov) performs the seduction dance of the *Habañera* for his Carmen (Zizi Jeanmaire). Here the *Habañera* can be identified by its context, by the music and one single phrase, *L'amour*. At the same time, this unique version stretches consistency to a point of tension, via the variability of exchanging genders. It is not Carmen who performs the *Habañera* for Don José. It is not Carmen and Don José who exchange places, as in the Saura version. It is Don José alone.

The Japanese video production of *Carmen*, directed by Makoto Sato (1989), has engendered a different kind of transformation. On the background of minimalist, expressive frames, mainly in white, red and black, a feminine voice-over talks about her relations with a man. The soundtrack is composed of a mélange of atonal music and selected themes from Bizet's opera. The libretto is entirely omitted but Carmen's fragmented inner monologue is suggestive of it instead. Musical themes from the opera are heard in various places throughout the film. Variations on the *Habañera* are played slowly on stringed instruments as she awaits her man. She thinks (voice-over): "I don't know his name, I don't remember his face" – while dancing with another man and while lying beneath the flowers after being stabbed by the first man. The final words are hers, murmuring in voice-over about her misunderstanding: "What did he try to do? What did he want to tell me? I can't understand. All I know..." Sato suggests a poetic investigation of a familiar situation in which a woman waits for a man, meets another man, the first man also meets another women but still wants the first one. He murders her out of possessiveness. This version, at least, gives Carmen what, for the most, she has been deprived of: her voice, her thoughts and her fears.

V   The Transformations of *Carmen*

All the examined transformations of Carmen involve three parameters: (1) the medium (technology, prestige, uniqueness of each medium); (2) repetition vs. originality (aesthetic norms); and (3) the question of gender roles (cultural norms). But it is this last issue that dominates most of the film versions of *Carmen*, downgrading the issues of technology and aesthetic norms. A good deal of technical, aesthetic and cultural changes have taken place in the cinematic institution over the years as *Carmen* keeps circulating in the cinematic bloodstream. Yet, within this chain of repetitions, there are two consistent elements. First, in various ways Carmen is deprived of her *libretto, music* and *gestures*. Second, only a very few versions suggest a different denouement, other than her death, i.e.: Chaplin, Reiniger, Janson, Dyer and Amadori, and all of these are either burlesques or parodies, occasionally in the form of a show within a show. All the other versions end with the death of Carmen.[15]

Significantly, in some of the examples discussed above, the gender of the performer is reversed. Both Saura and Petit play on gender, turning Don José into the one who dances for Carmen's, and the audience's, pleasure. At the same time, by gradually erasing the presence of the words, even so-called "postmodernist" versions reproduce the listening pleasure of the opera.

In this inquiry, evidences are mainly circumstantial (or textual if we like); however, the cumulative effect of version after version indicates a certain tendency. Technically, the cinematic medium has the possibilities to deliver Carmen's words on the screen. But, in fact, the diachronic re-reading and rewriting of *Carmen* through *gesture, music* and *libretto* have, in the course of more than a hundred years of cinema, been delineating another story.

Like Carmen in her *Habañera*, Olympia's hand positioning and direct look in Manet's painting "conveys at once greater inhibition and a more deliberate provocativeness."[16] In a gesture of concealment poised between address and resistance, Olympia takes the initiative and thus threatens the traditional imaginary control. Culture, in reaction, tends to portray and re-portray the two women, Olympia and Carmen, who transgress social roles. In this context, we may identify the *Olympia* series as a painted version of *Carmen*, as a family member of the *Carmen* series, and especially of the *Habañera*.

It is not surprising then that the visual composition of the "seduction scene" in Townsend's MTV version (2001), echoes the *Olympia* series: Carmen Brown's/ Beyoncé Knowles's body positioning and attire – recumbent on a sofa and wearing a transparent silver-colored gown and woven silver slippers – rewrite Manet's nude *Olympia*. However, Carmen Brown merges the figure of Olympia with that of her dark-skinned handmaid. As in Picasso's painting (1901), she is the black feminine figure who outrageously takes the place of the white Olympia in bed, this time as the provocative seductress. The fact that Carmen is deprived of the *Habañera* reveals not only aesthetic modifications in these obstinate repetitions but also, involuntarily, a social narrative where the cinematic institution keeps telling us about a female figure who challenges social conventions and dies as a result. (For Townsend's and MTV's *Carmen: A Hip Hopera* see ill. IV b, c, d)

Notes

1. On Townsend's *Carmen: A Hip Hopera,* see two papers presented at the Carmen conference held in Newcastle upon Tyne (2002). The first, by Susan McClary, introduces features of musical fusion in both Bizet's opera and Townsend's version and the second, by Abimbola Cole, focuses on the image of Carmen as a 'bad girl'.
2. In Clément words, 1989 (1986).
3. Tunes from the *Habañera* then become the subject of several auto-quotations by the opera itself (through the device of repetition). They are also the most quoted and familiar tunes of the opera.
4. Foucault remarks that Manet's *Olympia* was: "Perhaps the first 'museum' painting, [one of the] first paintings in European art that were less a response to the achievement of Giorgione, Raphael and Velasquez than an acknowledgement (supported by this singular and obvious connection, using this legible reference to cloak its operation) of the new and substantial relationship of painting to itself, as a manifes-

tation of the existence of museums and the particular reality and interdependence that paintings acquire in museums" (1977 [1969]: 92-93). From Clark's point of view, the painting represents a pivotal moment in the transition from one paradigm of art to a new one, one which has since dominated the art of the twentieth century (see Wollen 1980: 15).

5. See Furman, 1988 and Clément, 1989 (1986).

6. Spivak (1981, cited in Young 1990) has identified the three systems of domination active in colonization/class, racial/ethnic and sex/gender systems. These are all present in Manet's *Olympia* in a dialectical fashion. See also the discussion in Mieke Bal (1993) and Anat Zanger (1993).

7. Libretto by Henri Meilhac and Ludovic Halévy. Translation in the opera book of Bizet's *Carmen*, performed by the *Orchestre National de France*, 1989, conducted by Seiji Ozawa, with Jessie Norman. Furman (1988: 177) cites these lines and notes: "Carmen switches to the first person after the impersonal third person of the aria's first lines."

8. The restored version I studied was made from DeMille's personal nitrate print.

9. Chaplin might have used live/recorded music in the theater (see Tibbetts, 2004: 3), but on the level of the libretto: the words never appear, even in the film's graphic titles. At least, this is true for the version I studied at the Library of Congress Archive, Washington, D.C. and the videotape produced by Orbitfilms in their screen classics series. In this production the soundtrack of music accompanies Chaplin's film but this is definitely not Bizet.

10. The subversive use of inter-titles is "my enunciation" here.

11. In this sense it follows in the tradition of the *Opera-Comique*, which is responsible for the fact that there was so much dialogue in Bizet's *Carmen*. See Batchelor, 1984: 37.

12. Laura Mulvey, 1975, links the voyeuristic gaze to the pleasure mechanism of the male spectator in cinema.

13. Batchelor, ibid.: 36.

14. Another way that music appears in the film is through the subplot of the string quartet, but the music here is mostly that of Beethoven.

15. As for Binger and Nesna's film from 1919 (CARMEN OF THE NORTH), only the American version has a happy end.

16. Theodore Reff, 1977: 58.

Chapter 4
Masks

A fetish masks the absence, but not hermetically or permanently.

Hamid Naficy (1993: 97)

"She was lying, señor, as she always lied. I wonder whether that girl ever spoke one word of truth in her life" (Mérimée, 1963 [1845: 24]). With these words, Antonio (Antonio Gades in Carlos Saura's film CARMEN [1983]) presents Carmen – one of the most famous Romani figures in the world – to his dance troupe. He is not only quoting Don José's words from Mérimée, he is also creating an analogy between the old story and the new one. In this version Carmen is a dancer in the troupe who is playing the lead in the show while he himself plays the role of Don José, both on the stage and off. Time has passed and yet Carmen the gypsy is still depicted by a man, in this case one man quoting another.

Step by step, Antonio tries to examine the myth, but as he tries to change it, he is, in fact, repeating it. The confluence of repetition and difference is a strategy used in Saura's version, as in numerous other filmic variations of *Carmen*, to mobilize an old story for a new configuration. However, it is the dialectic between the "old" and the "new" that keeps producing additional versions. In this sense, the re-signification of *Carmen* is part of a cultural process of assimilation, appropriation and transformation, which also includes the act of reading itself.[1] Thus, from the present (and limited) point of view of this specific historical-cultural moment, we may identify *Carmen* as an emblematic cultural object that reflects the need to redefine the "I" and the "other" vis-à-vis law and desire.

I will argue that the Carmen figure, as gypsy and woman, functions as a source of both attraction and dread to society. This is, in fact, the motor which generates the plethora of remakes. In this respect, every new remake arouses the same apprehension: will the new version succeed in treading that same thin line that allows us to see Carmen and her gypsy band with both dread and delight? Can the new version succeed in maintaining the balance achieved so far – a balance that enables us, the viewers, to both accept and reject the *Carmen* story?

In this chapter I will discuss the textual procedures that enable the cinematic institution to "eternalize" *Carmen*. Like the socio-cultural systems of literature and opera before it, cinema uses a number of devices to deliver – persistently – a highly selective representation of Carmen and the gypsies and their Romani culture. Among these devices are a borrowed, "objective" discourse, a preference for indirect characterization, the "fluid" ethnic identity of the "other" and the production of a dialectic movement between legal and illegal space. Jean Baudrillard has suggested that as soon as the "other" can be represented, it can be appropriated and controlled (Baudrillard, 1983, in Young, 1990: 142). And metonymic representation is a way of controlling the stereotype. It is my contention that the corpus of the *Carmen* story is nurtured by dreams, desire, fear and fantasies of freedom and control.

Before turning to the texts themselves, I would like to discuss in some detail the role of stereotype and fetish that underlie the cinematic representations of Carmen. In the context of the endless chain of *Carmen* rewrites I will use Homi Bhabha's reading of Edward Said (1979) on the dualism at the heart of Orientalism:

> It is, on the one hand, a topic of learning, discovery, practice; on the other, it is the site of dreams, images, fantasies, myths, obsessions and requirements. It is a static system of "synchronic essentialism," a knowledge of "signifiers of stability," such as the lexicographic and the encyclopedic. However, this site is continually under threat from diachronic forms of history and narrative, "signs of instability" (1990 [1986]: 77).

The chain of Carmen versions and adaptations seems to be an exemplification of the way in which cinematic discourse embraces the tensions between the secure synchronic images of the "other" – including dreams, desires, fears and obsessions – and the dangerous changes, potentially encapsulated by newer versions yet to come. The presence of Carmen in its various representations, primarily in Western culture, is framed and constrained by "signifiers of stability": generated by repetitive practices of transparency that obfuscate the colonialist discourse of Carmen's textual enunciation, ensuring the transmission of the gypsy from one version to another as an object without a narrative or a history. This is accomplished, firstly, through encyclopedias, synopses, and program notes that rehash the desired contents; and, secondly, through the stereotypical representations transmitted from one film to the next. The reading of these various versions one against the other, however, potentially provides us with the ability to expose narrative features drawn from that other store – the "signs of instability."

As a cultural sign *Carmen* seems to have at least two options for survival. The first is to develop a history and a narrative. The second is to be transformed into a stereotype, or a fetish, by repetition. A stereotype functions in a similar way to a fetish which in Hamid Naficy's words "arrests in time and space a certain configuration of knowledge about the fetish object, the colonized" (1993: 98). As a form of multiple and contradictory beliefs, the fetish or stereotype gives us access to an "identity" that is based as much on mastery and pleasure as it is on anxiety and defense (Bhabha, 1990: 202). Hence, within this repetitive ritual, the figure of Carmen, her background and cultural environment, are concealed and denied. This is accentuated by the fact that most versions of Carmen were produced by white males.

I   Borrowing Objective Discourse

The entry "Carmen" in the *Larousse* encyclopedia gives the plot of the opera as follows: "For the love of Carmen, a gypsy, Don José, who is a corporal in the dragoons, deserts and becomes a smuggler. Ultimately, he murders his mistress who had left him for a matador." This synopsis, articulated by the editors of the encyclopedia, has often been reproduced, with additional details, in theater or opera program notes (Furman, 1988: 171). In *The Romantic Agony*, Mario Praz discusses Carmen as one of the many *femmes fatales* whose "diabolical feminine fascination" brings about a "violence of passion that makes the man lose regard for his own social position" (1970 [1951]: 207, quoted in Furman, 1988: 171). Nelly Furman suggests that the story could just as well be told from *Carmen*'s perspective:

> To thank him for letting her escape, Carmen, a Gypsy, bestows her favors on José, a corporal in the dragoons. He falls in love with her, abandons the army and joins the gypsies. When Carmen tires of him and his jealousy, breaks off their relationship and becomes involved with a matador, José kills her (1988: 170).

But, as Gayatri Chakravotry Spivak (1985: 129) says, "the subaltern cannot speak." Thus, the tale of a gypsy woman who has been loved and murdered by a white man is enshrouded not only in "objective discourse" – a practice which assigns to a certain discourse the aura of truth – provided by encyclopedias, synopses and program notes, but also in that other kind of "objective discourse" – folklore, tourism, geography and linguistics – used by the texts themselves.

Charles Vidor's film THE LOVES OF CARMEN (1948) exemplifies the "objective discourse" used in the representation of the Gypsy people. In two consecutive sequences, the gypsies are shot from what might seem at first sight two different perspectives: the "spectacular" and the "ethnographic." The first sequence presents the colorfully-dressed gypsies and Carmen (Rita Hayworth) dancing at Lillas Pastia's tavern to the music of the *Seguidila*.[2] In this scene, taken from

Bizet and recurring time and again in the cinematic versions of Carmen, the gypsies, with Carmen in the center, are participating in a spectacle for the visual entertainment of the white male. The next scene is a parallel representation of the gypsies, this time in their own encampment. Out of doors, near the bonfire, the gypsies start dancing "spontaneously." A young girl is singing while the others encourage her – until Carmen arrives and joins in. A few minutes later, the toreador appears, singing, and the crowd follows him. In this extra-textual "staged authenticity," however, no words are spoken and nothing is added to what we already know. This "ethnographic" sequence is presented as an opposition to the "touristic spectacle." But actually, as a form of objective discourse both sequences create another "signifier of stability" for the gypsies.

II   The Traveller's Gaze: Indirect Characterization

Mérimée cites Palladas in his epigraph: "Every woman is bitter and is only good twice – once in bed and once in death." This "ancient wisdom" has been reflected in the many cinematic versions made ever since. Carmen has become not only an erotic object for the voyeuristic gaze of both the spectators and the male protagonists (Mulvey, 1975) but has also been murdered over and over.[3]

According to the penetrating logic of the conqueror, Mérimée posits at the center of his novella an archeologist, scientifically equipped to expose the deep layers beneath the visible ones. He meets Don José and Carmen, and via a flashback arrives at the core of the story where he exposes the true nature of Carmen and the gypsies as the "black continent" of his mission.[4] Whereas the narrator functions as the center of consciousness in most of the story, this function is given over to Don José, a young white man from Navarre, during his confession. Carmen herself has no access to unmediated or direct speech. Neither do members of the gypsy band she lives and works with – including Carmen's husband, the one-eyed Garcia, Dancaire and Lillas Pastia. Nor are any of their thoughts and dreams ever represented in the novella's discourse.[5] This tradition has also been followed by the cinematic institution.

In the versions of *Carmen* made by DeMille, Lubitsch, Walsh, Christian-Jaque, Vidor or Rosi, the voyeuristic cinematic apparatus gazes at Carmen as she is dancing, seducing, cheating, betraying, and being murdered. Around her, always as secondary *catalysts*, are the Gypsies: their functionality is "attenuated, unilateral, parasitic" with regard to the main events and actions, to use Barthes's terms (1977 [1966]" 94). Playing cards, cheating and smuggling, the Romani are repeatedly framed with colorful, coin-decorated kerchiefs, vests and outsized earrings, very often appearing as cultural hybrids.[6]

In Mérimée, Don José's last words are: "Poor girl! It is the Calé [one of the Romani groups] who are to be blamed for having reared her as they did" (1963 [1845]: 66). The novella concludes with a didactic epilogue about the gypsies, thus shifting the focus of responsibility from Don José's character to the Romani, as if Carmen's fate were inevitable, bound to the gypsies' dark hair and dark eyes, their expression as of a wild beast, and their lives spent in filth, fortune-telling, and cheating. Though not expressed as such, Mérimée's "observations" have trickled down subliminally into almost all film versions. This attitude toward ideological minorities – ethnic or gender – is inscribed in the variations on the ethnic "other" as well as in the production of space that is structured around a legal/illegal dialectic.

III   Placing and Re-Placing Ethnicity

The ethnic variations at play in the cinematic versions of Carmen exemplify Teshome Gabriel's observation that "the screen is like the painted mask [...] in both there is exchange between absent-present and between representable-unrepresentable" (1990: 505). Gypsies are replaced not only by other whites on screen, but also by "others," such as American blacks, Japanese, and Senegalese. The first link, however, in Carmen's carnival of masks is Bizet's opera. It was Bizet who gave Carmen its first ethnic twist.

Temporal, spatial, musical and casting devices assisted Bizet in transmitting Carmen stereotypes as "signifiers of stability," all suitable for the operatic medium and easily adapted in turn by cinema. Bizet's "non-existent Spain" (Biancoli, 1953: 75) is mediated through an exotic mélange of gypsies and toreador figures, including a repertoire of "ready-made" musical motifs such as the Habañera and the "Toreador Song."[7] Bizet has not only eliminated the figure of the archaeologist-narrator, but also that of Carmen's Romani husband, Garcia. On the other hand, he has added Micaëla, Don José's mother's messenger and the white female alternative to Carmen. By reshuffling gender and ethnic hierarchy, Bizet seems to emphasize the interaction between the two minorities, the feminine and Romani. Micaëla, in contrast to Carmen, is not only "the virgin versus the whore" (Furman, 1988: 173), but also the white versus the dark woman. Micaëla, white and a woman, simultaneously constitutes both "center" and "periphery," identity and alterity.[8] Later, Preminger will produce Carmen, Don José and Micaëla as blacks (USA, 1954), and Robert Townsend will use the same transformation in Hip Hopera (USA, 2001). Kinoshita (Japan, 1951) and Sato (Japan, 1989) will make the protagonists Japanese. Chaplin (USA, 1916), Godard (France, 1983), and Brook (UK & France, 1984) will make them white.

Instead of three men romantically involved with one Romani woman, as in Mérimée's plot, Bizet's Carmen has a rival and Don José has another romantic option. Alas, Don José chooses the wrong woman and the wrong side, and for this he has to pay. There is yet another layer to this transgression. From the beginning "we face a world divided according to gender" (Furman, 1988: 174, paraphrasing Maingueneau, 1984). Don José penetrates the cigar factory, which no man is allowed to enter. Carmen, on the other hand, uses a knife, thus exhibiting supposedly masculine behavior. Clément's observations regarding Carmen are also pertinent here: "She threw down the flower ... the way knights used to throw down a glove. The gypsy's first transgression: she takes the initiative in lovemaking" (1989 [1986]: 50). For this she must be punished.[9]

Carmen, as the subaltern by gender, ethnicity and class, has to be re-inscribed in a subject-position different from that of Don José. Formulated already in Mérimée and Bizet, this principle is repeated "inaccurately" in films – under specific social restrictions, prohibitions and taboos – in a ritual that both examines and constitutes the norms.

DeMille's and Preminger's "inaccurate repetitions" (to use Judith Butler's term, 1993) might serve here as an example of the devious ways in which the cinematic institution imprints its changing scale of preferences in the reconstruction of minorities. DeMille's version (1915) revolves around the famous diva, Geraldine Farrar, who had played Carmen at the Metropolitan Opera in New York. On the one hand, DeMille exploits Farrar's renown and the highbrow cultural status of opera. On the other, DeMille's gaze photographs Farrar's white body as a mimicry of the gypsy's sensual body, thus expressing simultaneously a feeling of dread of and attraction for the "new woman" who challenges Victorian definitions of femininity (Higashi, 1994: 23). In CARMEN JONES (1954) Otto Preminger relocates the plot to the United States of the 1950s and replaces the original libretto with an adaptation by Oscar Hammerstein II in which the boxing ring becomes the *corrida*.[10] Preminger's intertexts are the genre of the American musical but they also adhere to the segregation code that had been approved by the American Supreme Court that same year. By substituting one minority for another, Preminger has shifted the white colonial gaze from the gypsies as Europe's "interior other" to America's notable "other." Thus, the "spontaneous" singing scenes of "Dat's love," "Dere's a café on the corner" or "Stan up to fight" are reminiscent of Vidor's "ethnographic" scene, but this time with American blacks.[11]

Worth mentioning in this context is the updated version of the MTV's *Carmen: A Hip Hopera*. While quoting from Bizet's opera, and using Preminger's version as its black intertext, black American director Robert Townsend suggests hip-hop as the musical register for the black American. Yet Carmen Brown and the main protagonists of Townsend's film are depicted as signifiers without a narrative or a history. These three American versions, made by two white males and one black one, conceal the interracial relationship between the main protagonists. In DeMille, "racial cross-dressing" takes place between the manifest and actual level of casting. Preminger and Townsend, in monochromatic versions, express ambivalence towards minorities; first, by replacing one minority with another and, second, by textual practices that deny the African-Americans their own voice. In these versions, white men are no longer "saving brown women from brown men" (Spivak, 1985, in Young, 1995: 152). The struggle of "whiteness" over authority, however, leaves its traces indirectly when gender and/or class replace racial differences.[12]

This is also the case in the free adaptations of Kinoshita, Chaplin, Reiniger, Amadori, Godard and Ramaka, where Romanis become Japanese, American, Spanish or Senegalese.[13] By positioning the main protagonists on the same East/West axis as the owner of the gaze (= the camera, the director), the gap between colonizer and colonized seems to be reduced. Is it possible that "West" and "East" no longer need the "other" in order to define themselves?[14]

In any case, despite the restrictions on interracial relations, the dialectic between desire and law is still maintained and inscribed at various enunciation levels of the films. Thus, in Godard's version, race is replaced by class when a lower-class Don José (= Joseph) finds it difficult to measure up to Carmen, a well-educated film director. Furthermore, Godard symbolically comments on the center of consciousness of the story when he replaces the narrator figure from Mérimée with Carmen's lustful uncle, a dysfunctional director (played by Godard) who has hospitalized himself in a mental institution. Another option on the gender scale was recently suggested by Matthew Bourne in the English ballet version, *Car-Man* (2001). Here, Carmen's body is used as the site of both attraction and distraction for homo-erotic desire. In the French-Senegalese version by Gaï Ramaka, on the other hand, Carmen herself experiences love for a woman. But here too the celebration of feminine desire ends with the traditional denouement, that is, death.[15]

In one of the few *Carmen* films made by a woman, Lotte Reiniger (1933) uses black silhouettes in her short black-and-white film to represent the various figures in the story. In this way, not only does she avoid the representation of interracial relationships but also the stereotype or "typical encapsulation" (in Said's terminology, 1979: 58) of the gypsies. Furthermore, her Carmen charms the bull with a flower, wins the toreador and gets herself out of the arena smiling. Three years later, Anson Dyer produced his short animated answer: *Carmen*. In this patriotic English version Carmen is charmed by Don José himself, who succeeds against all odds in overcoming the bull and the bullying toreador. Both versions, made in Europe between the two world wars, follow Carmen's fantasy of freedom without punishing her. Yet in Dyer's film, Carmen's freedom is eventually curbed by her loyalty to "her soldier."[16]

The re-signification process in the *Carmen* corpus is dominated by concealment, displacement and condensation in which gender and ethnic minorities mask one another. The borders – sexual, gender, national, race or class – are constantly being redefined, but the engine that keeps the story moving is the desire for that unfamiliar, "petit" object, that which the "other" seems to possess. The identity of this "other" may change, but not the mechanism of desire itself.

IV   Space and the Smuggling Gesture

The spatial dimension in cinematic versions like those of DeMille, Christian-Jaque, Vidor, Kinoshita, Rosi and Brook reflects a certain social order.[17] Taking their cue from Bizet's spatial conception, these films locate the actions on the axis between culture and nature and between the legal and the illegal. According to the spatial language of *Carmen*, love between Don José and Carmen may exist only outside the law. The first part takes place in town, where Micaëla, who comes from the village, seeks Don José among the soldiers stationed there. The village represents innocence, the childhood of Don José. The town suggests a different and less innocent socio-economic order. Here Don José comes to know that not all women have "blue skirts and long plaits falling over their shoulders."[18] The tavern, the location of the second part, is a liminal setting where two worlds meet: that of the soldiers and that of the gypsies. This is where the municipal and civil orders encounter the savage order of the third part, in the mountains, where the gypsies live outside the law. The fourth and last part reinstates the town, but now reflects a conflict between order and disorder. The crowded square symbolizes the borrowed time of carnival and the arena, where the toreador arrives with Carmen, and represents the realm of exile to which Don José will now belong (see Maingueneau, 1984). The cyclic movement of equilibrium, its violation and its restoration is thus produced by the "timeless space" (Said, 1979) of the many opera productions and cinematic versions that use the opera as their main source.

Within this context, I would like to pinpoint a key scene in the cinematic corpus: the smuggling scene. It is usually introduced by the scene in which Carmen offers to use her feminine powers in order to charm Don José and make it possible for the gypsies to smuggle in their goods. As far back as DeMille (1915), a gate in a brick wall in the middle of nowhere is guarded by a soldier. Carmen first meets Don José there, charms him and tries to persuade him to allow her

Romani friends to pass through the gate. She kisses him and he lets them through with their merchandise. Chaplin's A BURLESQUE ON CARMEN, as a manifest rewriting of DeMille, includes the smuggling scene, as do Dyer's, Vidor's, Christian-Jaque's and Rosi's versions. With or without a convoy of donkeys, the Romani people are always portrayed carrying bundles, boxes and baskets – an image of their "permanent circulation"– through the gate under Don José's nose.[19] Neither the merchandise itself, however, nor the place the gate leads to become known. Sometimes the gate is located near the sea and sometimes it is in the mountains. In all instances, however, the wall and its gate are continually policed and access is denied or permitted according to the guard's reading and interpretation: Who is allowed to pass through? What is their identity? Moreover, what kind of border does this gated wall stand for? And, how does all of this relate to *my* interests? (For De Mille and Chaplin see ill. II a and II b)

The vagueness of both the borders and the merchandise suggests that there may be a different kind of "smuggling" going on here. *Carmen* contains two kinds of space, each belonging to a different social order. The wall and the guarded gate exist in order to separate the civilized and structured "white" world from the nomadic life and open spaces of the Romani people. The tension between the two is expressed in the opposition between the uniformed soldiers, marching in orderly formation against the subversive, undisciplined gypsies.[20] The clash between the two worlds is seen in the robberies, looting and killing carried out by the gypsies when they ambush convoys of citizens traversing unprotected areas as they move from one place to another. In accordance with the nomadic principle, as described by Deleuze and Guattari (1987 [1980]), nomads' survival is dependent upon their ability to scatter over open spaces, settling for short periods of time anywhere conducive to eking out a living – in the mountains, the desert, the wilderness. When they run into a settled area that restrains them, they attack.

It is not only the physical danger, however, that is so menacing to the settled population, but the customs and beliefs that are also smuggled in – conveyed, communicated and disseminated by the invading nomads. Because what is really disturbing about the "others," in this case the gypsies, is the way they organize their pleasure: their excess of desire, their exaggerated enjoyment in the smell and taste of food and exhilarated dancing and singing, their strange habits and their relation to work (Žižek, 1993). In this respect, "the Giana, cigarette girl, thief, tramp, seducer and victim" (in Starkie's words) is emblematic of the Romani "other."[21]

If the political function of borders is to regulate civilized society in the face of such "others," it is no wonder that walls are erected between the two. Borderline areas refer to the transitional zones within which boundaries lie (Prescott, 1987). They create a kind of "third space" (Bhabha, 1990 [1986]), special in that it belongs to neither side but is an "in-between" space between two polar positions, one in which unexpected things happen, in which sparks are ignited. One of the characteristics of this in-between space is the element of surprise: the moment when something routine is *interrupted* and something new emerges – *a displacement* (in the Freudian sense), resulting from the impossibility of the encounter (Bhabha and Burgin, 1994: 454). It is at such a moment that Carmen – as an agent of dissolution – first emerges, heralding the cancellation of restrictions and limitations on the law.

V   Conclusion or "Will the Marvelous, Beautiful Story of Carmen Live Forever?" (Chaplin)

The traveller's gaze, the "pseudo-objective discourse," the indirect and partial representations by stereotypes, the simultaneous fear of and fascination with the "other" and the denial – all are components of the ritual of *Carmen* repetitions. Driven by a fantasy of control the repeated portrayal of Carmen and the gypsies on the screen is intriguing in two parallel practices: first, by the alternating ethnic identities of Carmen and the gypsies and, second, by the smuggling gesture.

As to the first, the changes from the Roma minority to black, white or Asian suggest a shift in the center-periphery dynamic. Carmen doesn't have to be a gypsy in order to be a "demonic *femme fatale*" or "a slave of her own will" (and to be punished for it). At the same time, this fluidity of ethnic identities functions as a "projective identification" (Mathijs van de Port's term in Iordanova, 2001: 214) in a way that redefines the border between white and colored people.

As for the "gesture of smuggling," it seems to function as a pocket of resistance to hegemony. However, by including the smuggling gesture as well as the punishment of those involved in the act in the diegesis, the cinematic corpus reassures us of what Emmanuel Levinas has defined as "the imperialism of the same" (1969 [1961]: 87). Hence, the act of smuggling also belongs largely to the discourse of those telling this story.

This can be found in Mérimée's novella: first, in the murder of Carmen, which occurs when the narrator is absent – as if the murder had committed itself – and second, in the anxiety arising from the reports of cultural contagion by Mérimée in his epilogue.[22] He reports not only on the various sources of the Romani languages but also on the presence of Romani words and expressions used by French thieves. At last we have it! The "contagious" quality of alien contacts cannot be fully controlled; the "germs" have already been "smuggled" into Western culture. In this way, we may identify the murder of Carmen as well as

I
Women running against the soldiers in Francesco Rosi's *Carmen* (1984)

II a
Seduction and smuggling in Cecil B. DeMille's *Carmen* (Geraldine Farrar) (1915)

II b
Seduction and smuggling in *A Burlesque on Carmen* by Charlie Chaplin (1916)
with Edna Purviance

III a
Carmen (Laura del Sol) and Antonio/Don José (Antonio Gades) in Carlos
Saura's *Carmen* (1983)

III b
Carmen (Dorothy Dandridge) in Otto Preminger's *Carmen Jones* (1954)

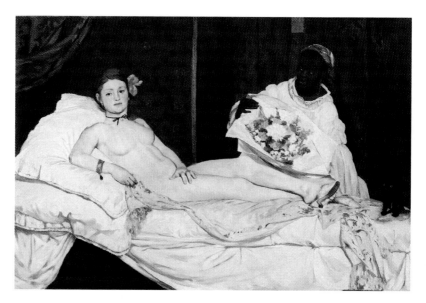

IV a
Manet's Olympia

IV b-d
A rewriting of *Olympia* in MTV *Carmen: A Hip Hopera* (2001)
with Beyoncé Knowles as Carmen Brown

V a
The opening sequence from Hithcock's *Psycho* (1960)

V b
The opening sequence from Gus Van Sant's *Psycho* (1998)

VI a

Joan of Arc (Jareldine Farrar) in Cecil B. DeMille's *Joan the Woman* (1916)

VI b

Joan of Arc (Jean Seberg) in Otto Preminger's *Saint Joan* (1957)

VII a
Accusations and the trial in Victor Fleming's *Joan of Arc* (1948)
with Ingrid Bergman

VII b
Accusations and "the trial" in David Fincher's *Alien III* (1992)
with Sigourney Weaver

VIII a
Jeanne d'Arc (Milla Jovovich) in Luc Besson's *Joan of Arc (The Messenger)* (1999)

VIII b
The death scene in Rosi's *Carmen* (1984)

that of Garcia, the officer of the dragoons, and the deaths of the toreador and Don José as acts of "disinfection."[23]

Using the trope of smuggling, it is possible to retell the *Carmen* story as a travelogue, which leaves a trail of smuggled/unacknowledged "goods" along the borderlines of Western and non-Western identity. Smuggling in the *Carmen* corpus has become not only a gesture of the Roma but also of the numerous interpreters and performers who keep retelling the story time after time. By smuggling into *Carmen* fetishes and stereotypes nurtured by both desire and fear the force of the myth continues to hold sway. Could it be that the gesture of smuggling itself, which sets in motion both scenarios of freedom and control, is what seduces us emotionally to consume yet another version of *Carmen*?

The desire for hermetic and impermeable borders repeats itself in various ways at the enunciation level of the cinematic versions, but Carmen, as a *displacement* of gypsy culture, is always knocking at the gate. Could it be that the next version will present a cinematic writing of the "other" story, this time as told by a Romani woman?

Notes

1. Space limits the possibility of expanding the discussion of competing historical explanations and changes in the status of the cinematic medium in order to contribute to our understanding of the remaking of *Carmen* at specific moments in history.
2. Worth mentioning is the fact that, according to the *Patrin Web Journal – Roma (Gypsies) in Culture and the Arts* (2001: 1), Rita Hayworth is of Romani origin (URL: http://www.geocites.com/Paris/5121/culture).
3. With exceptions in Chaplin, Reiniger, Janson, Dyer and Amadori.
4. See Freud on the roles of the psychoanalyst and the archeologist in *Gradiva* (1907); see also Ella Shohat (1993: 57).
5. Carmen is described only through the eyes of two men – the narrator and Don José – and their descriptions echo one another.
6. Discussing the Gypsies' presence as a minority in Balkan films, Dina Iordanova notes that most of the cinematic texts featuring the Roma continue to be made by non-Roma filmmakers (2001: 223). Elsewhere she notes that even Tony Gatlif, who usually tells stories about his Roma people, adopted, in *Gadjo Dilo* (1997), the Western gaze of a young Frenchman to tell the story of a Romani settlement (2000: 152).
7. See also Herve Lacombe (1999) on exoticism in opera.
8. Western women exist in a relation of subordination to Western men and domination towards non-Western men and women, according to Shohat (1993: 63) in her study of gender and the empire.
9. See Elisabeth Bronfen (1996 [1992]) on Carmen and the sacrifice of women.
10. For a discussion of *Carmen Jones* and ethnic differences see also Nelly Furman's paper "Carmen in Black & White" presented at The Carmen Conference held in New-

castle upon Tyne (2002). On the dubbing of Dorothy Dandridge's, Joe Adams's and Harry Belafonte's singing voices by professional and, in some cases, white opera singers in *Carmen Jones* see Jeff Smith (2003).

11. Jeremy Tambling (1987) remarks that *Carmen Jones* is "a mythologizing of the dangerous black or mixed race woman, and of her ambivalent 'nature.'" It further accepts the status quo (ibid.: 31).

12. On whiteness, see Homi Bhabha (1998).

13. It is worth mentioning that according to *The Patrin Web Journal* (see note 5 above), Charlie Chaplin claimed to be of Romani origin.

14. The historical and cultural explanations might be explored in a more extended study.

15. For a discussion on *Karmen Geï* see also Phil Powrie (2004).

16. As we have noted earlier, films like those of Chaplin, Janson or Amadori re-frame the story as a show within a show. These versions, all made during or between the two world wars, emphasize the tension between the fantasy of freedom symbolized by Carmen – who transgresses against law and convention in the show, and the rule of law that dominates the world outside. In this context Reiniger's and Dyer's films are two further examples that follow the fantasy of freedom.

17. On the spatial and social order, see Henri Lefebvre, 1991 (1974).

18. In Mérimée's text, Don José uses these words during his confession to describe the daughter of a Navarre farmer (1963 [1845]: 35).

19. See Irit Rogoff (2000: 37) on luggage.

20. It is worth mentioning that in Andalusia, where the story takes place, a *carmen* is a villa or country house, located between town and country, between culture and nature (Furman, 1988: 174).

21. In Walter Starkie (n.d.), p. 1.

22. The epilogue was a later addendum written by Mérimée in 1847, and not all the editions of the novella include it. See for example Nicholas Jotcham in Mérimée, Prosper: 1990 [1989]): xviii.

23. Depending on the version, some of these deaths or murders may not be presented in the films.

Part Two

Second Variation: Joan

Chapter 5
The Game Again

Joan of Arc was born in Domrémy in 1412 and was burned at the stake at Rouen at the age of nineteen, after only one year of public activity. Despite having been in the public eye for such a short period, Joan has excited the collective imagination for more than 500 years. The myth of Joan of Arc, or its "intellectual object" (Foucault, 1972 [1969]), has been engraved in the collective memory and is represented in encyclopedic sources, history books and biographies, and in other cultural texts and artifacts such as poems, sculptures, plays, tapestries, children's literature and even comics.

This process of re-articulation has been epitomized in at least forty films, including those of Georges Méliès (JEANNE D'ARC, France), 1900; Albert Capellani (JEANNE D'ARC, France), 1908; Cecil B. DeMille (JOAN THE WOMAN, USA), 1916; Carl Dreyer (LA PASSION DE JEANNE D'ARC, France), 1927-28; Marc[o] de Gastayne (LA MERVEILLEUSE VIE DE JEANNE D'ARC, France), 1928; Gustav Ucicky (DAS MÄDCHEN JOHANNA, Germany), 1935; Victor Fleming (JOAN OF ARC, USA), 1948; Roberto Rossellini (GIOVANNA D'ARCO AL ROGO, [JOAN OF ARC AT THE STAKE], Italy), 1954; Otto Preminger (SAINT JOAN, USA), 1957; Robert Bresson (PROCÈS DE JEANNE D'ARC, France), 1962; Gleb Panfilov (NACHALO [LE DÉBUT] [THE GIRL FROM THE FACTORY], USSR), 1972; Werner Herzog and Keith Cheetham (GIOVANNA D'ARCO, Germany), 1990; Jacques Rivette (JEANNE LA PUCELLE, France), 1993; and Luc Besson (JOAN OF ARC [THE MESSENGER], France), 1999.[1]

I will argue, however, that Western culture has never really digested the Joan figure. By recurrently authorizing new versions of the story, each of which allegedly provides new historical or textual evidence, Western culture has revealed its inherent ambivalence toward Joan's "initial story."

The story has troubled Western culture over centuries of memory, concealment and repetition, functioning as a "black hole" – a repository into which society funnels its inescapable terrors. Thus, while the Joan story is repeatedly produced, Western culture has cultivated a rigid set of norms for the purpose of subduing it and ensuring that it will be delivered in an "appropriate" manner. It is my contention that the key to understanding the eternal ritual of repetition can be found in the story's genealogy or, if we like, in the web that has produced the myth as it is told and retold, first by Joan's testimonies and then by those who recorded and interpreted it. The twisted object that has been framed by this apparatus is my subject of interest.

In this chapter I will trace the repetitions of the story as captured in the cultural memory of the 20th century, especially in encyclopedic discourse and the cinema. Identifying the "source(s)" of the Joan story and its main narrative units, I will offer a close reading of some of the most popular representations of Joan of Arc in encyclopedic entries. *Grand-Larousse, Britannica, Everyman's* and *Americana* all emphasize the characteristic detours that cultural tradition has constantly woven into what become Joan narratives.[2] These devices and detours are signals of a *censored discourse,* authorized again and again by the cinematic institution and its recipients.

I   Histories

Reading culture/history's attempts to tell the Joan story as a narrative (to emplot it, as Hayden White [1974] would put it) shows that it is structured like a relay race. The torch (= story) is passed from one agent to another with the express purpose of retrospectively changing the face of history. The act of rewriting, the most prominent featre of this process, is characteristic not only of the receivers of the story, who become, in turn, its senders, but also of the story's own initial phase. Exhibit 1: The trial of Joan of Arc is the first link in this successive chain, and its "sin" (i.e., rewriting history) was extensively explored in the rehabilitation trial, 25 years later. But this second trial itself was an act of rewriting, and it is the one that motivated the whole sequence of the transformations of Joan of Arc in Western culture.

The story of Joan of Arc exists in several official versions and in numerous unofficial ones. *Primary sources* include documents from the lifetime of Joan and her contemporaries.[3] *Secondary sources* include encyclopedic surveys, historical research, biographies and other cultural texts and artifacts. The distinction between the two, however, is rather tenuous. The chief "primary" sources in this case are transcripts of verbal reports of the proceedings against her and reports of her retrial. Additional information is provided by contemporary chronicles, letters and public documents. But the records concerning Joan's life are partial and fragmentary. The transcripts of both trials have shortcomings. The text of the first trial is written in the third person and "the only complete text is in Latin [...]. Occasionally even the Latin record is elliptical, indicating that some connective discussion or question has been omitted" (Gies, 1981: 3). The rehabilitation trial was based on evidence by witnesses required to recall events that had taken place 25 years earlier. To symbolize the validity of the retrial, a copy of the earlier proceedings was burned (Pernoud, 1955).

In order to trace the main components of Joan's story, a distinction should be made between the necessary elements – the primary names, places and events that function as the nuclear lexicon of the text (*the strong collection*) and the optional elements – the secondary names, places and events, which may or may not appear in all of the sources (*the optional inventory*) (Barthes' terms, 1986 [1967]).

As we shall see, the strong collection is foregrounded or emphasized, firstly through rhetorical devices and secondly by constant repetition in almost all of the sources. Yet it is almost impossible to create a singular syntax out of the lexicon, for there are too many options, too many unknowns. As for the optional inventory, its function in the Joan story is not the usual one of integrating the different cardinal points because too many options are being proposed (Barthes, 1977 [1966]). Furthermore, history must seem to *tell itself* in order to maintain the referential illusion, as if linguistic existence is merely the copy of another, anterior existence (Barthes, 1986 [1967]: 139). Quotations and explications are used as part of the "evaluation" procedure to mark the central points of the text (in Labov's sense, 1975 [1972]). Encyclopedic discourse has also developed a unique device to preserve continuity at any price – even when real continuity is lacking: a special lexicon is used in order to eliminate gaps (see, for example, Rüsen, 1987: 89).

The existence of the necessary components of the story has been established and reinforced through the *repetition* of an inventory of places, names and events: Domrémy and the voices; Vaucouleurs and its commander Baudricourt; Chinon and the Dauphin Charles VII; Orléans and Dunois; Reims, the march, the cathedral and the crowned king; Paris, the failure and the captivity in Compiègne; the Anglo-Burgundian alliance; Rouen with its inquisitors and commanders; Cauchon and the Earl of Warwick; the long trial and martyrdom, the retrial and the canonization process. All of these places and events are mentioned over and over again in the historical sources, in encyclopedias and in various cultural texts.

But many questions still remain and hence the components of the optional inventory are too many to list in full, but a number of them will hint at the uncertainty of the story: the nature of Joan's voices; the versions of her testimony; the power that seduced Charles to follow her and, more specifically, the secret exchange between them at Chinon; Joan's official rank in the army; the number of soldiers under her command; the events at Beaurevoir; Joan's leap from the tower; Joan's abjuration and relapse; Joan's death, including her brothers' query: Did she really die?[4]

II   Unattainable Mythemes

My analysis locates itself within the space created *unwittingly* by the text. Hence, in analyzing encyclopedic entries and cinematic texts I will pay particular attention to the rhetoric of the historical and sexual discourse. "Mythemes," in Lévi-Strauss's terminology (1979 [1958]), are the minimal units of the myth that carry significance. As a result of the unique relations between the three levels of discourse in the Joan story – the strong collection, the optional inventory and the rhetoric – three of the aforementioned mythemes play major roles: the voices, the dress and the trial. They recur again and again in every version of the story, either manifestly or implicitly. However, these three mythemes recur differently each time and take on many disguises, pointing to the "danger zones" of the myth.

The First Mytheme: The Voices

The voices that Joan heard are one of the most significant and yet enigmatic details in her career.[5] Encyclopedic sources use various options to present the same entity, especially in the segment that describes Joan's childhood and the revelation. According to the *Britannica* (1954: vol. 13: 72), "When she was 13, Joan first heard *a voice* from *God* assuring her of *Charles*'s right to rule, and commanding her to expel the enemy"(emphasis added). *Everyman's* states the case less categorically: "according to her own account," etc. While *Everyman's* specifies that the voices she heard were those of the saints Michael, Catherine and Margaret, the *Britannica* provides this information in a more detailed manner: "Among them [the voices] she distinguished those of Catherine and St. Margaret, who appeared to her in the guise of queens, wearing rich and precious crowns. Sometimes their coming was heralded by St. Michael." This source also adds: "Thereupon she vowed to remain a virgin and to lead a godly life." The *Larousse* quotes Joan's testimony about the frequency of her voices and the mission that was imposed upon her, emphasizing the cardinal function of the voices but without specifying their identity.

Joan's voices were the key to her gaining the support of her family, the chief of command in Vaucouleurs, the Dauphin Charles and his court, and the priesthood in Poitiers. They also influenced the commanders in Orléans, her captors in Rouen, her judges in the rehabilitation trial and eventually the decision of the pope to canonize her (Warner, 1979; Sullivan, 1999). Functioning as a "blank page," her voices were appropriated in each of the various tellings by a different authority who sought to inscribe upon them its own voice, thereby willfully dictating its meaning. The indeterminate nature of the voices enables her addressees to infuse their own meaning by positioning Joan as a mere go-between. According to Marina Warner (1979), Joan would describe the voices in spiritual terms to her friends and followers, but during the trial she was gradually maneuvered into a world of concrete sensation. The changes in her description of the voices during the trial are expressions of her inner conflict. During the stage of her desperation, Joan borrows attributes known to her from religious iconography: wings, crowns, etc. She now also refers to Saint Michael. With her positive reply to the question of whether she had ever kissed or embraced the saint, the trap has been laid. Her relations with the Devil could now be confirmed.[6]

Joan's own descriptions at the trial, as we can see, are the source of the multiple versions generated with respect to her voices.[7] This phenomenon has created a sort of *"version-en-abîme,"* that is, versions within versions and within the tradition of the many transformations of the story in Western culture. Also notable in this context is Joan's purported attempt to escape from Beaurevoir Castle, which became the subject of cross-examinations in both public and private sessions. "In the summer of 1430, Joan leapt from the tower of Beaurevoir Castle" (Warner, 1979: 113, based on Tisset-Lanhers, 1870). This is virtually "underground" information, not usually mentioned in the encyclopedias or in artistic renditions. It is worthy of particular attention due to the telling censorship. In the first trial alone, the incident is treated differently in the first and final drafts of the charges: "*In the first draft* of the charges, Joan is accused of boasting she would escape with the Devil's help" (Tisset-Lanhers 1870 [vol. 2]: 223 in Warner: 114, emphasis added). "But when the leap from Beaurevoir appears *in the final list*, her enemies' words cut both ways: she sinned by trying to kill herself, though she knew she should not, because her voices told her not to" (Tisset-Lanhers 1870 [vol. 2]: 329, 417, Warner: 114, emphasis added). Any account Joan could give, then, would necessarily undermine the authority of her voices and place her in the wrong: she would either have been obeying them, meaning they had to be of the Devil, or disobeying them, and thus committing the sin of suicide at her own initiative. She was thus forced to shift ground continuously in the course of the trial. This is why, in my view, it is Joan herself who is again responsible for reconstructing or, as it were, rewriting, the related events. Here again, *"multiversionality"* is part of the inner poetic logic of the story.

This fact, as well as the leap itself, has been silenced by cultural memory. The encyclopedias mention only that Joan planned an offensive at Compiègne, besieged by the Anglo-Burgundian forces. On May 24, the Burgundians took her prisoner. The *Britannica* supplies some additional details: "Joan, who had charged the enemy in an attempt to save her comrades, was left outside and was taken prisoner, together with her brothers and Jean d'Aulun. She was taken to the Burgundian camp" (1954: 74). After supplying some political evaluations, both *Larousse* and the *Britannica* mention that Joan was imprisoned at Beaulieuen-Vermandois, Beaurevoir and Arras – all in Burgundian territory. This apparently minor episode is condensed (as in Freud's dream work) in the *Britannica*, with the addition of some significant details: "She thought of nothing but the people of Compiègne, and after a long consultation with her 'voices' made an attempt to go to their assistance by jumping from the tower. She injured herself, but not seriously" (ibid.). Interestingly, it seems that suicide remains a taboo to this day. Five hundred years of Western culture have had to conceal her attempt to do so while repeatedly dealing with her persona.

The Second Mytheme: The Dress

The second mytheme deals with Joan's efforts to secure the support of the local governor. Woven between the lines, however, is the story of her dress. In 1428 Joan left home for Vaucouleurs, where she addressed herself to the local governor, Baudricourt. She asked him to supply her with an escort on her journey to meet Charles the Dauphin in Chinon.[8] In the *Larousse*, this segment of Joan's life is followed by background information about the complicated situation prevailing in France at the time. In the *Britannica*, the political situation in France functions as an explicator (to use Labov's term, 1975 [1972]) for Baudricourt's actions. The Vaucouleurs segment concludes with the explanation that Baudricourt cooperated with Joan after he learned about the serious situation in Orléans and Vouvray. The *Britannica* emphasizes that the journey was made without the knowledge of Joan's parents, an argument later heard against Joan at the trial.

According to Joan's testimony, in response to her plans, her father declared that he would rather drown her in the river (Tisset-Lanhers, 1870 [vol. 2]: 115; Barrett, 1931: 102-3, both referred to in Warner, 1979: 154). The *Britannica* also goes into detail about Joan's actions when Baudricourt sent her back to her parents: "The people of Domrémy retreated with their cattle to Neuf-Chateau, where Joan spent a fortnight with La Rousse who kept an inn" (1954: 72) and then goes on to explain that this "is the origin of the false Burgundian legend that she was a light woman, liking the company of men at arms" (ibid.). The last argument is reinforced by its juxtaposition with an apparently minor anecdote: "Some time after, she was summoned for breach of promise of marriage before the magistrates of Toul, by a young man who had sought her hand" (ibid.). Joan's chastity, then, is preserved: she keeps her vow; she gives up earthly love for her mission. This is certainly put in a roundabout way. Does the digression signify something more? If we skip the next paragraphs in the *Britannica* – which deal with the political atmosphere in France as Joan waits for Baudricourt to authorize her journey – we come across another clue: Baudricourt sent Joan "on a horse dressed in a male garment" (both in the *Larousse* and the *He-*

brew Encyclopedia, 1963, vol. 16: 893, my translation). The *Britannica* adds: "The people of Vaucouleurs brought her a horse and Joan exchanged her suit of red cloth for a page's dress" (ibid.).

At last we have it! The discourse resorts to a formal device of oppositional analogy in order to distinguish between the people's acts and their understanding and Joan's acts and her understanding. While they simply bring her a horse, it is Joan who initiates the change of dress. Here we have a new story, smuggled in through the Vaucouleurs event: that of Joan's revolt against her father's will or, if we choose, against the patriarchal order. It has three stations: the escape from home, the rejection of marriage and the transformation of dress. This pattern is typical of a tradition of stories about disguised female monks (Warner, 1979: 150-2).

Throughout her transvestism, she abrogated the destiny of womankind [...]. [...] by never pretending to be other than a woman and a maid, she was usurping a man's function but shaking off the trammels of his sex altogether to occupy a different, third order, neither male nor female, but unearthly, like the angels whose company she loved" (Warner, ibid.: 145-6)[9].

At a time when women were barred from independence, from self-expression, from public action, says Warner, Joan appears to have used her voices as a channel to achieve all of these. The sin of Joan of Arc is the violation of a severe taboo: a declaration, through appearance and action, of her will to engage in masculine affairs. While the encyclopedias evade or marginalize these problematic issues, they cannot obliterate the traces of their centrality, which surface in the list of charges brought against Joan in court.

The Third Mytheme: The Trial

The story of the trial was worked and reworked in court, and fashioned into the guises we already know. The end of this circular story is contained in its beginning. Since whatever we know about Joan's life is based on her testimonies and those of her contemporaries, the story we think we already know is the story we will never hear.

The sources concentrate on the circumstances of the trial.[10] The *Britannica* supplies information about the tribunal, which, "skillfully selected by Cauchon, consisted of ten members of the University of Paris, strong Burgundians and intolerant theologians, 22 canons of Rouen, all completely in the hands of the English government" (ibid.: 74). The *Larousse* points to the violation of rules in Joan's imprisonment: "*Contre toutes les règles en usage dans les procès d'inquisition, [elle] était détenue en prison laïque et gardée par des geôliers anglais, et non par des femmes dans la prison de l'archevêché*" ["Contradicting all the rules governing inquisition, [she] was held in a prison staffed and guarded by English men and not by women as in the archbishop's palace"] (ibid.: 343). The *Britannica* sums up the twelve main points on which the judgment was based:

> They include the opinion of her judges as to the worthlessness of her visions and her different accounts of the sign given to the king; they denied her gift of prophecy, censured her masculine dress, her disobedience to her parents, her attempt to escape and the sinful pride that had led her to believe that she would go to Paradise and that she was responsible only to God and not to Church, which the judges represented (ibid.: 74).

And it adds: "The last offense was that which chiefly incensed the theologians and led to her condemnation" (ibid.).

With respect to the accusations, the *Larousse* cites one of Joan's most famous and most frequently quoted answers: "*Êtes-vous en état de grâce? Si je n'y suis, Dieu m'y mette, et si j'y suis, Dieu m'y garde*" [Are you in a state of grace? If I am not, God will place me in one, and if I am, God will keep me in it"] (ibid.: 343). But this pure and at the same time sophisticated answer did not satisfy the court. The central goal of the interrogation was to incriminate her at any price. The leading rationale of the accusers relied on the belief that the Devil's demonic entity might disguise itself through a heavenly appearance. It was only the Church that possessed the knowledge and the authority to recognize the Devil's presence (Tisset-Lanhers, 1870 [vol. 2]: 63, Warner, 1979: 101).

The subject of her dress was raised innumerable times, both prior to the trial and during it, and tied to her refusal to renounce male dress and return to the realm of womanhood, as ordained by the Church. The charges were that "the said Joan put off and entirely abandoned women's clothes, with her hair cropped short and round in the fashion of young men, she wore shirt, breeches, doublet, with hose joined together [...] and other arms in the style of a man-at-arms" (Barret, 1931: 152-4, cited in Warner, 1979: 143).[11] The *Larousse* tries to justify Joan's choice of male dress by supplying practical reasons: she dressed like a man in order to defend herself from her English guards. But, as Warner notes, Joan did not specify any practical reasons for her dress until the very end of the trial. Her abjuration on May 24, 1431 and its reversal show how strongly she cared about her dress. As indicated by both primary and secondary sources, on May 24 Joan was taken to the cemetery of St. Quen in Rouen, as part of the interrogation process. Present on this occasion were Pierre Cauchon, the English and Burgundian prelates, the cardinals of Winchester, the Duke of Bedford, the governor of Rouen castle, the Earl of Warwick and other of her enemies. History, however, suggests a variety of ways to read this scene. The *Britannica*, describing Joan's vindication and subsequent denial, writes:

> These facts are known only by means of a nonofficial report, annexed to the minute of condemnation. They bear, however, the stamp of probability, and it is certain that

Joan regretted her momentary and easily understood weakness in the tumult of the cemetery of Saint-Quen, with the thought of the stake before her (ibid.: 74).

And whereas the *Britannica* tries to reduce the distance between the probable and the certain, the voice of uncertainty prevails in the various accounts of the retrial in which the official version is questioned: "Was Joan, who could not read, tricked into signing a document of recantation, which disavowed far more than she realized?" (Pernoud, 1955: 177-82). Various witnesses proposed that the documents were switched at the last moment, pointing out that Joan signed a short declaration whereas the abjuration, as it appeared in the trial records, is very long. (Warner, ibid.: 140).

Since Joan – the chief witness at her own trial – presented so many versions of her life story, the official discourse has created its own versions. Encyclopedic sources, which serve as the main recorder of collective memory, frequently choose, each in its own way, to follow only one fork of each narrative junction, while censoring the others. The heterogeneity of the story is denied in favor of an apparently homogeneous and monologic text, which confirms conventional mores.

III   Regime of Discourses

The need to legitimate a different version of the events each time stems from the heterogeneous nature of the sources themselves, creating a kind of *"versions-en-abîme"* and, consequently, a sense of uncertainty regarding central elements of the myth.[12] Cultural memory tries to censor the real drama behind its rhetorical curtains, but this drama is visible in the inner logic of the story, constituted by a multiplicity of versions and threatened by disconnected paragraphs, omissions and displacements. These symptoms of censored material reveal the web that frames the sign. Since the desired object is the "origin" or the "source" of the myth, the movement of repetition promises by its very nature the pleasure of reproducing the lost object of desire. The story of Joan of Arc throughout history is governed by a cultivated tradition that produces a "doxa" of what and how this story is permitted to be told. I understand the ancient Greece notion of doxa as common knowledge and shared opinions, "all that is considered true," and that, according to Barthes, "is a major obstacle to individual thinking" (in Ruth Amossy, 2002: 1)

Joan has been portrayed repeatedly for more than five hundred years: she is the impious daughter and pregnant witch in William Shakespeare's *Henry VI, Part I*; she is a sexually desirable patriot in Chapelain's long poem, *La Pucelle, ou*

La France déliverée: Poème Héroïque en Douze Chants (1656), where Dunois is depicted as falling in love with her; she is the subject of Voltaire's parody, *La Pucelle d'Orléans* (1760), which uses Chapelain's poem as a pretext for casting doubt on her virginity; she is the "Maid" in Friedrich Schiller's tragedy *Die Jungfrau von Orleans* (*The Maid of Orléans*) (1801), where she is presented as falling in love with an English soldier; she is viewed through the imaginative eyes of her page in Mark Twain's play *Personal Recollections of Joan of Arc, by the Sieur Louis de Conte (Her Page and Secretary)* (1896); and she figured in the twentieth century as a social Amazon in Bertold Brecht's *Die heilige Johanna der Schlachthöfe* (*Saint Joan at the Stockyards*) (1929–1930). Joan is a political victim in the struggle for secular power in George Bernard Shaw's play, *Saint Joan: A Chronicle Play in Six Scenes and an Epilogue* 1924)); and she is the enigmatic figure in the existentialist trial in Jean Anouilh's play *L'Alouette* (*The Lark*) (1953).[13]

Alas, it makes no difference from which side we look at the story, we are caught forever in the dialectic that drives this enigmatic story and keeps it alive in the minds of its receivers: saint or witch? patriot or androgyne? The phenomenon of polar opinions for and against Joan has not changed over the centuries. On the one hand, French chronicles like *Chronique de la Pucelle* and *Journal du Siège d'Orléans*, written shortly after Joan's death, represent what might be called a providential viewpoint. They, along with Christine de Pisan, the famous feminist poet, assume or imply that Joan was sent by God to save France and Charles. On the other hand, we have hostile Anglo-Burgundian chronicles of Joan's lifetime that inspired many later texts, including Shakespeare's. In 1921, one year after her canonization, the English anthropologist Margaret Murray, in her *Witch Cult in Western Europe*, declared Joan to be a witch (see Gies, 1981).

The dominant principle behind the inventory of plots that Western culture has to offer for the story is an everlasting trial where she is condemned again and again. The voices that she heard, the men's clothing that she wore and the men's roles that she performed – in all of these things Joan was trespassing on territory forbidden by the taboos of the Middle Ages and by the tenets of the Christian Church. She was crossing the culturally fortified line that separates between men and women.[14]

In the wake of the multiplicity of historical "sources" on the one hand and the problematic issue of Joan's sexuality on the other, a rather rigid tradition emerged on how to tell the story while remaining within the confines of propriety. We may conclude that all the retellings of the Joan story comprise a history of the various attempts to deny its heterogeneity and reduce it to a homogeneous system. Nevertheless, the inner core of the story – its heterogeneity and diverse femininity – is smuggled into the history of culture from generation to generation. Thus, each new manifestation seems to prove that Western culture has never really been able to digest Joan of Arc.

Marina Warner describes the changing stereotypes used in different cultural periods to represent the figure of Joan in successive chronological terms (1979). According to Warner, the telling of the Joan story has been limited to a so-called heroic discourse: "The life and death of Joan of Arc have been told since 1431 according to ancient laws of narrative in the West: the hero must die before his time" (1979: 273). Joan appears under the motto "a heroine for all seasons," (ibid.:), changing according to evolving social and cultural needs (from knight to Amazon to patriot). My own view is that Joan's image has always been dominated by the problematic of the story itself. Hence, the discourses and stereotypes created around Joan of Arc are more complicated than the hegemony of the "heroine for all seasons." In differing with Warner's heroic, chronological model, it is my contention that Western culture utilizes at least two different types of discourse *simultaneously*, in order to deal with the problematic story.[15]

The first kind is *neutralized discourse*, which avoids the problematic of Joan's sexual identity by attributing to her the ready-made traits of holiness, nationalism, heroism, or an inclination to political conspiracy (as in the texts of Péguy, Shaw, Brecht and Anatole France). A favorite cliché, typical of this sort of discourse, is treating Joan as if she were a man (a knight, saint, or patriot) – although externally she remains a woman. Given the centrality of the charges regarding Joan's refusal to wear women's clothes, such discourse is merely avoiding the issue of her distinctive sexuality. The second type, *romantic discourse*, presents Joan as if she were, after all, "only a woman." She has human/womanly feelings, and might potentially fall in love with Dunois, Lionel or even Charles VII. She experiences inner conflict (ideals versus human needs) and may reject her lover (as in Chapelain) or become pregnant (as in Shakespeare). Schiller's play is an example of a text that makes use of ready-made items from romantic discourse, in this sense. But it also borrows attributes from the patriotism that originally belonged to the first, heroic, order of discourse, and adapts them to a different purpose, reinforcing the inner conflicts of the heroine. Both neutralized and romantic discourse, though expressed differently, have the same goal: the first tries to circumvent the issue, the second to provide an artificial solution.[16] As emphasized in Voltaire's parody, Joan's virginity (and androgyny) is the soft underbelly of the legend, but also its nucleus.

Within the framework of this tradition, the history of cinema boasts over 40 different versions of the Joan story (thus far). Interestingly enough, some of the film versions of the Joan story have suffered a similar fate to that of the primary sources. Several, like Capellani (1906) and Caserini (1908), have disappeared entirely; others have been restored and "improved." Cecil B. DeMille's JOAN THE WOMAN (1916), for example, was shortened by DeMille himself and then reedited by the French during the First World War. Dreyer's film LA PASSION DE JEANNE D'ARC (1927-28) was first censored in 1928 by the Archbishop of Paris for its villainous depiction of church officials, re-created with sound by Lo Duca (Gaumont Production, 1952) and restored in 1981 when a print was found in a Norwegian mental hospital.[17] The cinematic versions began to join the long tradition of cultural manifestations associated with her even before her canonization in 1920. While this proliferation of versions would seem to offer the promise of finally revealing the truth, the whole truth and nothing but the truth, it seems that the truth has a different disguise each time and the multiplicity of versions is still based on what has been solidly developed by tradition. The rules of the game require that the new medium keep playing around Joan's refusal to buckle under to the dictates of the social order and to punish her while simultaneously relocating her in that same social order.[18]

Cinema has joined the tradition, but it has also developed its own specific attributes. The repetitive selection of representational modes in the different cinematic versions has created an arsenal of attributes among which three types predominate: hagiographic, patriotic, and clinical-romantic. The first type, hagiographic discourse, can be illustrated by George Méliès's Jeanne d'Arc (1900) or Marc[o] de Gastyne's La Merveilleuse Vie de Jeanne d'Arc (1927), for example. Both hagiographic texts emphasize Joan's spirituality through her physical appearance and the physical presence of the voices, avoiding any disturbing evidence of either her problematic sexuality or the existence of political confrontation. The second type, patriotic discourse, is exemplified by Cecil B. DeMille's JOAN THE WOMAN (1916) and Victor Fleming's JOAN OF ARC (1945), both of which were produced and released in wartime, the former during the First World War, and the latter immediately after the Second World War. Both DeMille and Fleming highlight representations of a ruined and divided France, detailed battle scenes and political intrigue.

Both hagiographic and patriotic discourse function, however, as neutralized discourse, which aims to legitimize Joan's contribution by concealing her personal conflicts under the veil of the traditional religious and/or secular orders. The third type of discourse, on the other hand, the clinical-romantic type exemplified by Otto Preminger's SAINT JOAN (1957), Gleb Panfilov's LE DÉBUT (1972), and Werner Herzog's GIOVANNA D'ARCO (1990), makes a much more complicated detour: while locating Joan within a traditional order (secular and/or religious), it also tries to legitimate her sexuality on the level of the romantic trajectory. The recognition of Joan's mental disturbance with its schizophrenic symptoms allows the clinical-romantic discourse to represent her as ill and therefore not responsible for her behavior.[19]

But there can be a fourth, *alternative*, meta-discourse. This category contains, as we shall see, versions like Jacques Rivette's JEANNE LA PUCELLE (1993) or Luc

Besson's JOAN OF ARC (THE MESSENGER) (1999). Its first and most notable member, however, is Dreyer's LA PASSION DE JEANNE D'ARC (1927-8). Like Foucault's heterotopic place, Dreyer's court is also a locus of crises.[20] If the suspect's attempt to reconstruct the past is a passport into the "symbolic order" of the court (see Feldman, 1991), Joan's failure to do so prevents her from becoming an object of legal discourse. However, the impossibility of her participation in this ceremony enables her to preserve her past as an act and not only as a text (see Feldman 1991, following Deleuze and Guattari 1986).

After five and a half centuries of interpretation, the distinction between fact and fiction, reality and legend, is far from clear-cut, especially in this case where the blurring of distinctions was, and still is, an inherent part of the game of repetition. Cultural structures have dictated the repertoires available for selection in order to smuggle the story into history. At the same time, the classic Western narrative tradition has forced itself to add void narrative functions (the optional inventory), simply to hide the scandal of the text's *heterogeneity*. This represents the only possible way of telling the story and, at the same time, of keeping its loose ends tied together.

Joan's diverse femininity is disguised in various ways beneath a homogeneous facade. Often, "her-story" is transformed from "history" to "hysteria." Nonetheless, when the authority of history is questioned, both heterogeneity and diverse femininity come into their own. As we have seen, the voices that Joan heard are one of the most significant and yet enigmatic details of her career. The next chapter will trace the various ways that Joan's cinematic biographies struggle with this constant and significant element within the context of the historical genre of cinematic biography.

Notes

1. According to Margolis (1990: 393-406), 38 versions had been produced till 1990. Margolis's account, however, includes also indirect versions like "The Story of Mankind" directed by Allen Irwin (1957) or "Joan the Ozuk" directed by Santly Joseph (1942). On the other hand, to her list one should add new film and TV versions made after 1990 such as those of Werner Herzog, Jacques Rivette, or Luc Besson. Other sources, such as *Cinémaction* digital data bases like IMDb and BFI, each present their own lists and numbers. For early versions see Pierre Leprohon, (1962).

2. I will use four of the most widely circulated international encyclopedias to analyze how the Joan story is reflected in the encyclopedic repository of popular memory: The *Encyclopedia Britannica* (USA, 1954), The *Grand-Larousse Encyclopédique* (France, 1984), *Americana* (USA, 1961) and *Everyman's Encyclopedia* (England, 1967). As will be shown, cultural memory is captured, and at the same time produced, in the encyclopedic reservoir.

3. These sources appear to be rich, abundant and diverse, a unique state of affairs for a medieval personage and rare for a historical figure of any pre-modern period (Gies, 1981: 2).

4. Joan's brothers claimed that someone else was substituted for Joan at the stake and that Joan herself continued to wander around France (Warner, 1979: 188).

5. "In Joan of Arc's case," says Marina Warner, "her historical image has been frozen at one with her voices: Joan never comes unaccompanied. Historians, artists, psychologists have had different ideas about her voices' character and origin and verity; some, though very few, think she lied about them; most sceptics hold that she believed in them but they had no objective reality. That Joan of Arc heard voices is nevertheless the fulcrum of her personality and the motive force of her story" (1979: 118).

6. See also Karen Sullivan (1999).

7. Marina Warner's illuminating reading in her *Joan of Arc: The Images of Female Heroism* (1979) and the various perspectives that she offers hold the key to a deeper understanding of the story and its status in Western culture. Nevertheless, this reading seems to employ rhetorical tactics to mediate and blur the many voices in Joan's story, as do the encyclopedias. Warner prefers to supply explanations that diminish the disquieting effect of the multiplicity of versions.

8. This information appears in both the *Britannica* (1954) and the *Larousse* (1984).

9. On Joan's sexuality and virginity see also Anat Zanger (1993, 2001), Carina Yervasi (1999) and Francoise Meltzer (2001).

10. Notable phases in the trial are: (1) 12 February-3 March 1431: Public session of trial; (2) 10-17 March: Sessions in prison cell; (3) 19 May: University of Paris condemns Joan; (4) 24 May: Joan's abjuration at the cemetery of St. Quen; (5) 28 May: Joan withdraws her recantation; (6) 29 May: Joan is condemned as a heretic, and handed over to the secular authorities for burning.

11. Karen Sullivan adds that: "The cleric's descriptions of Joan's choice of coiffeur and wardrobe supported their contention that she presented herself in such a way because she wanted to rather than because she had to" (1999: 47). According to Adrien Harmand (1921)"Joan had her hair cut in particularly contemporary style, trimmed in short bangs over the forehead and shaved above the ears and around the neck. Though she wore a relatively simple [...], she assumed far richer garments at later stages of her career." (In Sullivan, ibid.: 46)

12. *Versions-en-abîme* is a word play on *mise-en-abîme* and refers to the mirroring of the version within the sources.

13. Notable cultural manifestations of Joan of Arc, mentioned only in passing here, constitute an object of study for Raknem (1971) and Margolis (1990). Warner (1979) perceives the relation between text and culture as reflecting one another.

14. See also Deuteronomy 22: 5: "The woman shall not wear that which pertaineth unto a man, neither shall a man put on a woman's garment; for all that do so these are an abomination unto the Lord thy God." Cited in Warner (1979: 139).

15. Warner concludes that Jeanne is captured in the heroic tradition of the West that is handed down from generation to generation as a "stable monolith in an unstable world" (ibid.: 275). It seems, however, that there is a missing link in Warner's argument, as the shift from a chain of successive "ecotypes" over the course of culture to a monolithic view of discourse is not evident. Since the selection and admission of

the repertoire is culturally conditioned, differentiation may occur either synchronically or diachronically (see Even-Zohar, 1990 [1982], and McHale, 1986: 86-7). Thus, while relating to reflections of Joan of Arc in culture, we may distinguish between two levels: (a) a regime of discourse or discourses that governs the appearance of (b) which is comprised of different repertoires constructed by alternating ready-made attributions.

16. It is in this respect that we may understand also Robin Blaetz's observation that: "Joan of Arc's chief attraction may lie in the chance to pornographically depict the death of this potent female with chains, ropes and lascivious camera work" (cited in Joan Acocella, 1999: 103).

17. According to Pipolo, the Norwegian print of Dreyer's film is essentially the same as the Paris Cinémathèque copy (in Margolis, 1990: 39). See Richard Abel (1984: 196-9) and Tony Pipolo (1988).

18. A more elaborate analysis of the films themselves will be presented in the next chapters. On Joan of Arc in cinema see also Michel Estève (1962), Robin Blaetz (1989), Anat Zanger, (1993 and 2001), Olivier Bouzy, (1999), Carina Yervasi (1999) and Michaud-Frejaville (2001).

19. I am using here Mary Ann Doane's term of "medical discourse" (1986).

20. In his book on Dreyer's film, David Bordwell asserts that "La Passion de Jeanne d'Arc is one of the most bizarre, perpetually difficult films ever made" (1981: 66).

Chapter 6
Hearing Voices

> If we reverse the binary oppositions fact/fiction, presence/absence, the liberation of the fictive may generate new possibilities for the study of history.
>
> Edith Wyschogrod (1998: 27)

The more than forty cinematic representations of the story of Joan of Arc created during the last century offer us the possibility of examining the twists and turns of the "same" historical biography over an extended period of time. It would appear that Joan's life is a well-defined object, around which the cinema has created its own choreography of changing reflections. But, in fact, the story itself already contains tension between events and their representation. Joan, in her various testimonies, and others, at her rehabilitation trial, were – like historical cinema itself – recounting a reality no longer in existence. Furthermore, the historical and cultural memory of Joan is not a singular entity; it exists in a number of formulations, some of them contradictory.

Joan's life, as recorded by the cinema reflects the interplay between the various historical and cultural sources of her life, the changing conventions governing historical biography over the past five hundred years (the existence of at least 126 biographies of Joan attests to this [Margolis, 1990]) and the qualities inherent in the filmic image itself. Despite developments from the silent film to the digital, these qualities are one of the major sources of the complex relations between cinema and historical biography.

Using the corpus of Joan of Arc films as my example will enable me to trace the ways in which the cinematic institution maneuvers between cultural-historical memory and the conventions of the genre. By repeatedly creating new versions of Joan's biography, cinema has revealed a certain unease with the existing inventory of historical referents, and each new version purports to tell the "true" story, the story that has not yet been told. The concreteness of the cinematic medium produces a unique representation system for the historical referent. As we shall see, some versions try to conceal the limitations of their own knowledge, while others openly reveal them. In both cases, however, previous visual and filmic materials are used as if they too were historical referents.

Before considering the cinematic corpus of Joan of Arc, it may be useful to look at the notion of historical biography in the context of the photographic image. With its strong affinity to a reality that no longer exists, the historical biography would seem to compel the cinema to examine the qualities and limitations of the photographic image. It is no accident that the meta-historical novel has a certain affinity with cinematic and photographic models (McHale [1987]; Hutcheon [1989: 47]). Photographs and, later, films generated a crisis in the relations between reality and its representation. In this respect they function not only as symptoms of the phenomenon but also as its catalysts.

I   Image, Biography and History or *Let Us Now Praise Famous Men*

In August of 1936, *Fortune* magazine sent the writer James Agee and the photographer Walker Evans to Hale County, Alabama. For twenty-one days, they stayed in the homes of three average white tenant-farmer families in order to document the social reality of the United States during the Great Depression. The two, however, did not produce an ordinary journalistic report. Instead, Agee shared with his readers his agony in the face of the complex and elusive reality that was impossible to document. He attempted to give meaning to the lives of these poor cotton farmers through categorized lists, chapters and sub-chapters, subjects and sub-subjects, while presenting the documentarian as someone asking the wrong questions and using the wrong tools. Accompanying Agee's descriptions were Evans's black-and-white photographs – devoid of captions, dates or any other defining words. The photographs acquired more meaning every time the reader flipped back and forth between them and Agee's descriptions.

Their report was rejected by *Fortune* and only after several years was their work published as a book called *Let Us Now Praise Famous Men* (1941). Today it is considered one of the most important studies of American cultural history ever made. By stretching the borders of documentary prose and photography to the extreme, Agee and Evans bared the complex relations between reality and its documentation and, at the same between, between reality and art.[1]

That same year, Orson Wells's Citizen Kane was released. The film was received with critical approbation, not least because of the special photography employed, which made possible a simultaneous view of the foreground and the background in the same shot. But what made the film outstanding was the cumulative effect of the newspaper investigation which called into question the usefulness of its own investigation.[2]

More than four decades later, Woody Allen, in Zelig (1982), borrowed the devices of the documentary film in order to present the biography of an entirely fictitious person. He himself portrays Leonard Zelig, nicknamed Chameleon because of his habit of impersonating others. By doing this he metaphorically symbolizes the same phenomenon produced by the film. The quasi-documentary quality of the film is achieved through the use of segments of authentic newsreels from the 1930s and their accompanying anonymous yet authoritative voice-overs. These documentary materials are interwoven with fictive scenes, shot in the same visual style as the documentaries. Like the hero of his film, Woody Allen borrows qualities that are not his. He incorporates into his film historical characters like Heinrich Böll, Gertrude Stein and even Adolf Hitler, taping them onto the realistic level of the film. An ontological tension is created between familiar history and Woody Allen's history, as when he appears side by side with Hitler on the speakers' platform.[3] This tension underlies the viewing experience and makes us wonder about the power of the cinematic picture in constructing photographed history. The previous knowledge of the viewers vis-à-vis the director and the actors enables them to identify ZELIG as an image of reality without a source.[4]

All three texts mentioned here call attention to the ambiguous ontology of the image in historical biography. These biographies emphasize the capacity of photographs to be accepted as part of the documentation of reality, on the one hand, and the limited point of view of the observer, on the other.[5]

II   The Ambiguity of Historical Images

Discussing the varieties of the historical film, Robert Rosenstone (1995) has observed that conventional historical films make use of mainstream cinematic norms in order to present the "look" of the past. Three elements are usually used by the cinematic mechanism to do this: the photographic sign, the conventions of the genre and the realistic narrative. Within the framework of the historical film, these elements encourage us to view the cinema as "boundless memory" (Wyschogrod's term: 1998), memory that has recorded reality through the camera's lens and enables us to view it again and again.

Let us begin with the nature of the photographic sign. The accessibility of the image, resulting from the resemblance between the photographic sign and the referent, encourages us to make the transition quickly and, at times, even automatically. In his article on the photographed picture (1977 [1964]), Roland Barthes stresses that the message of the photograph is, first and foremost, "This is how it was." A movie, on the other hand, says: "This is happening now" (ibid.: 45). In this way, one can understand the tension between reality and its representation by words and stills in Agee and Evans's book and in the films of

Orson Wells and Woody Allen. Films and stills can be used, under certain circumstances, as evidence in a court of law. On the other hand, we know now that
developing technologies are able to produce artificial images of a reality that
never existed.[6]

As for the conventions of the genre of the historical film, its *differentia specifica*
is its strong affinity to the reality of the past. Non-fictitious films in general, and
historical cinematic biographies in particular, maintain a "double referential
mechanism" (Hrushovsky's term, 1982: 75). On the one hand, the films deal
with the areas of significance of the world constructed in the film: the characters, the events, concrete space. On the other hand, the areas of significance
being constructed are constrained by an external system of knowledge identified as "historical reality." According to this mechanism we judge the Zelig figure played by Woody Allen or Heinrich Böll as played by the figure himself.
The tension created between the world that the film constructs and the accepted
conception of historical reality plays a central role in designing the generic "con-
tract" of the historical film.

The third element used by historical cinematic discourse is the realistic cinematic narrative. In mainstream cinema the viewer is encouraged to identify the
film with reality. Among the factors contributing to this are the "invisible" editing of the film, the transparency of the screen, and the coherent narrative structure, all of which locate the viewer in the ideal position of "omniscient viewer."
However, the historical narrative, as emphasized by the three meta-historical
biographies examined above, contains *areas of uncertainty* – the inner lives of the
heroes and the inaccessible, multifaceted quality of the historical event (McHale,
1987: 87). Subjective experience or perspective poses a dilemma for cinematic
discourse: how do we know what we know?

The three elements of the cinematic mechanism discussed above point to the
paradoxical task facing the historical film. While writing, recording and shooting with a medium whose special strength is in recording "the here and now,"
the historical film is, in fact, trying to represent a reality that no longer exists.
The historical film must therefore create the concrete-real object and its representation as well.[7]

When we come to deal with the concrete-real object in the biography of Joan
of Arc, the areas of uncertainty extend, as we have seen, over a great portion of
what appear to be elements of her biography. Cinema, like other cultural media,
tells the story with the aid of an already existing narrative scheme such as saintliness, patriotism or political conspiracy (as in the texts of Bernard Shaw, Bertold Brecht and Anatole France), or romantic conflict (as in the texts of Shakespeare and Chapelain). At the same time, the cinema has developed its own
representational conventions. Two kinds of events in Joan's story seduce the
cinema time and again. The first is the result of the medium's hubris: the vast

crowded scenes describing the notorious battles of Orléans, Compiègne and Paris offer the cinema an opportunity to celebrate its technological abilities; it turns historical drawings into filmic spectacles, orchestrating huge numbers of soldiers, horses, armor, weapons, costumes, injuries and deaths. The second has to do with the areas of uncertainty, such as Joan's voices. The cinematic representations of these voices will be the main thread of my reading here. Joan herself described the voices ordering her to help liberate France that she had heard in her childhood, voices that continued to attend her throughout her life – but her descriptions of these voices *changed* during the course of the long trial as, under the pressure of the interrogations, her abstract descriptions became more and more concrete (see Warner, 1979: 118).

Identifying Joan's voices as an "anxious sign" enables me to explore its traces as they filter through the historical trial to inhabit different levels of cinematic representation, that is, in various developments of plot, in the figurations of the voices and in the physical representation of Joan herself as a woman who hears voices.

III   The Voices as an Anxious Sign

Preminger's SAINT JOAN (1957) can be used to illustrate the problematic status of the voices in mainstream cinema. In this film Charles's dream opens and organizes the narrative: Joan appears in the dream twenty years after her death, together with the spirits of Dunois, Couchon, Warwick and the English soldier who gave Joan a cross as she ascended the stake. The dream structure, as in the Shaw play (1920) upon which it is based, traces the friction between Joan and the social system. Joan desires to be resurrected even as the twentieth-century messenger brings the news of her canonization. But despite the conciliatory atmosphere of the dream-sequence, her request is rejected: the Church informs Joan that it prefers its saints dead. Working within the Hollywood tradition, however, the dream structure also supplies a realistic motivation for supernatural situations, and the conventions of Hollywood replace the principal drama, thereby turning the story into a melodrama of impossible love.

Joan's voices are represented in this film only through dialogues. Her declarations that she has heard voices and been charged with certain missions are greeted with suspicion by those around her, but when she succeeds in pulling off a miracle or two the usual response is, "She has been sent from heaven." The positioning of Joan as the ultimate "other" is developed gradually in the course of the film but becomes clear in the scene between Joan (Jean Seberg) and Dunois (Richard Todd), the military commander whose initial hesitation turns to admiration. The film, in the best Hollywood tradition, shows the two young heroes against a romantic sunset. After the coronation, Joan feels isolated at the royal court and seeks solace in the chapel. Dunois follows her, to the accompaniment of organ music:

> Joan: [...] Let me tell you a secret. Here, from the bells, I hear the voices.
> Dunois: *You make me feel uneasy when you talk about your voices.*
> [...]
> Joan (smiling): I wish you were one of the village babies.
> Dunois: Why?
> Joan: I could nurse you for a while.
> Dunois (smiling): *You are a woman after all.* (He puts his hand on her neck).
> Joan (resolutely removes his hand): No, I am a soldier, nothing else.[8]

These lines point to Joan's voices as the main barrier to an expression of her femininity. By rejecting Dunois's unuttered request, Joan chooses her truth and her punishment – meted out to her not only by the secular and religious orders of the Middle Ages, but also by the authority behind the screen in 1957.

The supernatural quality of the voices has constrained the filmic versions of the Joan story to use, abuse or bypass the conventions of historical biographical discourse in order to represent them cinematically. It is my intention to trace the various ways the voices are rewritten: first, in the films by DeMille and Fleming, which tend towards the traditional mode of historical representation and the "historical eventfulness" of the battlefield scenes (to use Sobchack's term, (1995 [1990]: 286)); secondly, in the films by Panfilov and Herzog and Cheetham which exhibit a more experimental approach towards the past; and, finally, in the films of Dryer and Besson, as examples of self-referential texts examining the cinematic historical discourse of Joan of Arc.

The narratives of DeMille and Fleming, like that of Preminger, are structured around a flashback that underlines the function of the film as the teller of history. Both DeMille and Fleming combine saintliness and patriotism, and both were made in the context of a world war (DeMille's in the middle of the World War I, Fleming's in the aftermath of World War II). I will begin with Fleming's JOAN OF ARC (1948), which has pretensions to being an authentic historical biography.[9] In the opening sequence, to the peal of church bells, the camera focuses on the ceiling of a church, the very church, explains the voice of the narrator, in which Joan was sentenced to death and, 500 years later, elevated to sainthood. The pages of an old Latin tome then fill the screen while the authoritative masculine narrator recounts the life of Joan of Arc in France of the fifteenth century, creating another dimension of time – historical time.[10] The events mentioned are accompanied by maps and dates that endow the film with the quality of a classic national documentary. (For De Mille's *Joan the Woman* and Preminger's *Saint Joan* see ill.VI a and VI b)

The spectator sees Joan (Ingrid Bergman) kneeling in front of an old chapel against the background of the ruins of Domrémy, and learns indirectly that her "voices" have ordered her to join the struggle to liberate France. Joan may be talking, but it is the disembodied masculine voice of the narrator that lends validity to the absent elements in the visual space (Joan's voices) and, at the same time, bypasses the issue of representing them. Later, having decided to renew the attack during the battles of Orléans, Joan tells the army commanders: "You have been with your counselors, I have been with mine." Here, too, the viewer learns about Joan's voices indirectly. The validity of her voices will become evident after Fleming films Joan leading the attack, holding the standard on high and being wounded, and then her rapid recovery and victory.

DeMille's silent film JOAN THE WOMAN (1916) primes the viewer to see Joan (Geraldine Farrar) as a national heroine. She is shown in silhouette on the background of France's national symbol, the fleur-de-lys. The subtitles present her as France's liberator from English rule. In the long battlefield sequence DeMille seems to combine the "historical eventfulness" of the battle scenes and the throes of Joan's inner conflict as she is forced to choose between her feelings (her love for an English commander) and her national mission. Familiar optional miraculous elements such as the breaking of Boudricourt's sword and Joan's rapid recovery from wounds on the battlefield are also included. Yet De-Mille's story is set within another frame, the story of a British soldier volunteering for a dangerous mission in World War I after seeing a vision of Joan of Arc fulfilling her patriotic mission. In a flashback to Domrémy, we learn that Joan has saved the life of an English soldier, Eric Talbot, played by the same actor playing the British soldier in the frame story, and the two fall in love. But as Eric declares his love for Joan before going back to the front, a blazing sword appears on screen and a messenger of God calls Joan to her mission. We actually see a visualization of Joan's revelation, while the message of the "voices" appears in the subtitle. During the siege of Orléans, Joan wakes up terrified one night because (as the subtitle tells us): "Somewhere French blood is flowing." This vision acquires its validity in the visuals of the next sequence when Joan decides to attack.

Unlike Fleming's film, which conceals the problematic identity of the voices by their indirect presence in the films, DeMille's film represents Joan's vision on the visual channel while her voices appear on the graphic channel of the subtitle. The device of presenting Joan's voices without a "voice" might be unavoidable on the basis of the cinematic technology at the time. However, despite De-Mille's overall traditional approach, the presence of the subjective vision of the floating sword together with the film's subtitle, Farrar's imperial presence, and the story of Joan's love affair with an English soldier, point to his interest in Joan's inner conflict.[11]

Unlike the films discussed above, Panfilov's as well as Herzog and Cheetham's films do not incorporate battles scenes. These are replaced by a metaphoric analogy in Panfilov's film and by the libretto and a decor with images from the field of slaughter in Herzog and Cheetham's operatic version. Here Joan's inner conflict is the main focus and the plot functions as an occasion to redefine feminine voices as well as cinematic historiography.

Panfilov, in LE DÉBUT (1970), describes the life of a young actress, Pasha, playing the lead in a movie about Joan of Arc (Inna Tchourikhova). It revolves around an impossible love affair between Pasha and a married man and an analogy between the affair and the story of Joan's life. Sequences from the film within the film, that is, the production of Joan of Arc, include familiar elements such as her capture and trial, her confession of guilt and her retraction, her wish to hear her voices again when she is in prison, and her being burned at the stake. At the same time, they include two scenes unknown from official history. In the first scene Joan wants to judge the male sex and even defend them, despite the objections of the (male) judges. In the second, Joan, wearing a white cloak, is leading a line of men dressed as knights through the darkness; she examines their weapons, one of the men asks for forgiveness, she refuses, another confesses that he is frightened but Joan orders him to continue, while a third man one mumbles, "Witch."

In this way, Panfilov uses a strategy characteristic of alternative history as it was used by postmodernist literature (see McHale, 1987: 87-9.) The imaginary trial of the judges is a fantasy that contradicts our collective memory of the story while turning one of its central foundations – the judgment of Joan – into the object of parody. The second scene militates against traditional historical discourse, which seeks to present Joan as a saint and patriot who won the complete faith of the soldiers despite the fact that she was a woman.

Herzog and Cheetham's GIOVANNA D'ARCO (1990) is based on the opera by Verdi and Solera (1845), which was in turn based on Schiller's drama (1801). Herzog and Cheetham chose to locate the story in primordial time and space. By doing this, they destroy the spectators' expectation of seeing a historical reconstruction of the Middle Ages. The stylized theatrical qualities of the decor, the dialogues sung to the score of the opera, the curtain that falls after every scene and the camera's subsequent focus on the applauding audience – all express the director's refusal to take part in the quixotic chase after a historical referent. Herzog's commitment is to the central elements of the story and to the conventions of the opera. The integration of opera and history here produces a metaphoric interpretation of a historical tale. In the opening scene, Joan is wandering through a dark forest while her father seeks her out, anxious to bring her home before it is too late. Joan's inner conflict is presented through two sets of voices, angelic and demonic, that she hears while asleep. The angels urge her to keep her faith in God and the heavenly afterlife. The demons try to tempt her into following her heart and her desires. When she awakens she finds a sword at her side. The conflict becomes more intense as Charles declares his love for her. In this respect, Herzog's operatic film version does not only focus on those areas of uncertainty in the story, such as Joan's inner life, but also gives the plot a romantic twist – as did the versions of Shakespeare, Chapelain and DeMille. Joan's essential struggle here is against the patriarchal order, represented by her father, the king, and the army, as well as against the conventions of opera which require the death of the heroine.

The films of Panfilov and of Herzog and Cheetham focus on areas of uncertainty and offer interpretations of unknown or unfamiliar events from the optional inventory of the tale. These events aim to illuminate, metaphorically, the past, and the way in which the past may be relevant to contemporary issues (see Ankersmit, 1974).

My last two examples, the films of Dryer and Besson, concern themselves not only with the Joan story but with the issue of what it means cinematically to tell a story that has multiple versions and an optional inventory.

In LA PASSION DE JEANNE D'ARC (1927-8), Dreyer's silent film purports to focus on the trial against Joan and its repercussions and is based on documents published in 1920.[12] Through the name of the film, its structure, and the fact that it supposedly deals with the last day of Joan's life, Dreyer seeks to create an analogy with the passion of Jesus. In fact, the film describes Joan's last weeks in Rouen, the endless interrogations, her confession of guilt and subsequent retraction, and her execution (Agel, 1985: 46). The inter-titles do not provide the viewer with any background or commentary about the events being viewed – only dialogue: the accusations, the comments of the judges and Joan's reactions. While traditional historical discourse is being provided by the inter-titles, the visual channel is undermining it and creating an alternative discourse.[13] As David Bordwell (1981) has noted, the film is divided into seven sections according to location and to a scheme of scenes that alternate between Joan's cell and outside of it: the court to the cell, to torture chamber, to the cell, to the cemetery, back to the cell and, finally, to the courtyard of the castle where Joan is taken to the stake. Each of the seven sections opens with some sort of dialogue between the authorities and Joan and her few supporters. Whenever there is disagreement, Joan is attacked. The screw is tightened at every turn and the effect produced is one of a conspiracy against Joan. The feeling is intensified by the incoherent narrative space achieved through the violation of the representational norms of traditional cinema. The pictures are flat, as if hanging in a vacuum. The characters are drawn from place to place within the frame and the camera seems to refuse to follow the movements of the characters with any consistency. The viewers are prevented from locating themselves at the center of action. The result is that the viewers identify with Joan and with her uncertainty and disorientation in the face of the relentless interrogators. In this way, Dreyer presents the court as a place of crisis in which the court proceedings are unable to capture the complexity of Joan's life. Her voices are present mostly in her refusal to share them with the hostile authorities. In Dreyer's film, the written words and the *mise-en-scène* are indicative, more than anything else, of Joan's distress. Everything we know is based on the trial. But the detachment of the written dimension of the trial from its photographic one points to the impossibility of ever coming into contact with the historical referent in Joan's case.[14]

Besson's 1999 film, JOAN OF ARC (THE MESSENGER) opens, like Fleming's, with a map of conquered France that emphasizes Vaucouleurs, Orléans, Chinon, Compiègne and Paris. But this time there is no narrator, only rhythmic sounds and subtitles describing France under siege: "Only one thing can save it; a miracle!" Besson attributes Joan's actions to a childhood trauma. Joan is seen as a young girl (Jane Valentine) intensely influenced by the church and experiencing religious visions. Lying in an open field, she sees, as we do, flashes of the messenger of God (a very young man) sitting on a stone throne, and discovers a sword at her side.[15] There is the sound of a rushing wind and a pack of wolves passes by. From a distance, one hears the beat of horses' hooves. The revelation scene combines elements of fantasy with elements of realism. The discovery of the sword symbolizes the initial stage of her mission and, as in DeMille's film, is connected with the occupation of her village. When she returns home, she discovers that English soldiers have burned and pillaged the village, and she is witness to the rape and murder of her sister – Besson's addition to the official historical narrative. At this point, Joan (now played by the older Milla Jovovich) accepts the mission conferred on her.

At their first meeting, Joan shares with the Dauphin her revelatory experience. As in the first sequence, the spectator sees flashes, including some in the shape of the messenger. His words, however, are uttered by Joan. Only during the battle does the spectator both see and hear the messenger himself. Besson incorporates a detailed sequence (over 40 minutes long) in which the cinematic machine joins forces with the war machine, presenting not only the liberation of Orléans but also the technical achievement of a huge filmic battle. The conflict between Joan as a woman and the masculine army environment is magnified here, overtly discussed ("Joan, you have to understand, we cannot take orders from a girl," says La Hire, a senior commander). It ends with the victory of Joan's voices, which guide her through the attack. Occasionally, "historical eventfulness" in this sequence turns into "hysterical eventfulness," as when

Joan acts impulsively and her struggle with her voices is observed by the masculine eyes around her. (For Besson's *Joan of Arc* see ill. VIII a)

Joan's voices are present during the battle in a few flashes that merge with the fighting. The spectators can actually see and hear Joan's "partner" in her inner dialogue. Unlike other versions examined here, Besson's visually unmasks the voices from the beginning of the film.[16] Like the "acousmatic voice" described by Michel Chion (1999: 18), the voice, whose embodiment has not yet been seen, seems to have omniscient power. Once we both hear and see the messenger, he loses his power in a process that might be called here the "de-acousmatization" of the voices (ibid.).

The revelation scene depicting the discovery of the sword and the battle episodes recur in Joan's last days. After a long interrogation she returns to her prison cell where she vainly awaits the voices that seem to have abandoned her. The messenger from God, now an older man, comes to test her beliefs – or perhaps it is only the voice of her conscience. He interrogates her on the scene in which the sword was revealed to her, offering her several options. Perhaps it fell from the hand of one of the cavalrymen passing through. Perhaps there was a battle and the sword was left behind. "Perhaps," he says, "you didn't see what you saw – you saw what you wanted to see." Besson suggests a cinematic investigation which, like Orson Wells's CITIZEN KANE and Joan's rehabilitation trial, calls into question the usefulness of its own investigation.

In a television interview (Pivot, France 1999), Besson remarked that what interested him particularly was why Joan insisted on continuing the war. The king had decided to end the fighting and the soldiers were exhausted. Besson found the reason in extra-historical events – in the trauma of her childhood. In the film, just before her death, Joan tells the messenger (her conscience, if you like) that she had seen "many signs, those that I wished to see. I fought in order to get revenge. Out of desperation. I was all the things that people believe it is their right to be when they are fighting for an idea." Besson thus emphasizes the *areas of uncertainty* in Joan's story, suggesting a psychological interpretation of some of the most important historical events.[17] In this way he also questions one of the most sacred foundations of cinematic viewing: to see is to believe. "Perhaps," he is also saying to the spectators, "perhaps you haven't seen what was, but what you wanted to see."

IV   An Intertextual Dialogue

My reading of selected versions of the Joan story revolves around the notion of historical referents, such as her voices, on the one hand, and the battle scenes, on the other, as they are recorded in the filmic material. Joan's cinematic corpus uses many items from the optional inventory, which result in the production of large areas of uncertainty – already present in the historical tale(s). Like other cultural media before it, the cinema has been seduced by the gray areas between fact and fiction and aims to give its answers through the use of its own materiality – the concreteness of the image, the concreteness of the voices and the relations between them. Concreteness is of major importance here: the abstract quality of the historical experiences of the voices has become concrete against Joan's will, while the concreteness of the cinematic sign tries to avoid concrete representation of the voices and suggests "historical eventfulness" of the battlefield instead. Like Joan's judges during the historical trials, the cinematic institution uses concreteness as a tool of understanding the voices, but by doing so the cinematic versions of Joan might be in danger of working against the conventions of the historical genre itself. The selected versions used three types of solutions in order to solve this dilemma: (a) concealment and partial representation (DeMille and Fleming, for example); (b) alternative history which suggests a metaphorical interpretation (Panfilov or Herzog); and (c) exposure of the impossible procedure of a concrete representation of the voices (Besson).

Through the elements of film language such as sound, color, costumes, actors and landscape – called by Rosenstone (2000: 186) "the other material" – the cinema endows the past with a concrete expression. The historical film implies that what is historical is a physical reality (as observed by Staiger, 1989, in Sobchack, 1995 [1990]: 294). But what happens when we view the same historical film biography again and again but each time it looks different?

The distinguishing constituent of the photographic sign, as explained by Roland Barthes (1977 [1961]), is the analogical connection of resemblance between the sign and its referent. In the historical sources there exists no visual documentation for Joan's physical appearance except a silhouette of her face during the trail (Warner, 1979: 13, Pernoud, 1994: 114). What, then, would be the correct cinematic choice – one that would personify the face and body of a fifteenth-century village girl who has excited the public imagination for hundreds of years?

The cinema as an audio-visual medium offers us the face of Joan, the shape of her forbidden body, and the sound of her voice as recorded and projected on the screen. The faces of Geraldine Farrar, Simon Genevois, Renée-Marie Falconetti, Jean Seberg, Ingrid Bergman, Florence Karrs and Milla Jovovich are added to the "technological memory bank" (Kaes, 1990) of Joan's portrait as a historical concept and as a cinematic icon.[18] The director's choice for the feminine lead is thus a significant element in the presentation of Joan's life and contributes to the ever-growing lexicon proposed by the cinema for the concept of Joan. In the history of this cinematic lexicon are faces that were temporary, easily forgettable, portraits of Joan, and there were memorable faces that we want to see again and again.[19] DeMille and Fleming chose well-known stars for the role. Fleming chose Ingrid Bergman, as did Roberto Rossellini for his own version of the story. But DeMille's choice of Geraldine Farrar was received with astonishment (Higashi, 1994: 133-4). What does the buxom prima donna of the Metropolitan Opera have in common with a simple village girl?[20]

The *double referential mechanism* usually operates in historical discourse to evaluate the "truthfulness" of historical events, places and figures.[21] In the cinematic sub-genre of Joan's historical biography, the referential mechanism leans on yet another layer of knowledge: the intertextual mechanism that points to the cultural and cinematic sign as a referent. The cinematic rewritings of a historical myth like Joan of Arc have been nourished by over five hundred years of history and culture. A familiar repertoire of "ready made" cultural and cinematic signs is waiting to be used. Changing stereotypes, images and plots are used in different cultural periods to represent the figure of Joan and to transmit the tale in already known narrative schemes. Thus, viewers will follow these films vis-à-vis their "horizons of expectations."[22]

Another look at Besson's version will show us how this film, too, makes a contribution to the rich reference lexicon of Joan of Arc through cinematic quotations: Milla Jovovich, who had played the feminine lead in Besson's THE FIFTH ELEMENT (1997), carries over to her subsequent portrayal of Joan traces of the lost fight between good and evil in her previous film.[23] Like DeMille, Besson includes Joan's vision during the siege of Orléans as she awakes, terrified, seeing "French blood flowing everywhere." Like DeMille and Fleming he includes Joan's injury during the battle and like Fleming, Besson's Joan says to the army commanders: "You have been with your counselors; I have been with mine." When the battle is over, Joan, as she had in Fleming, expresses her deep pain at the sight of the wounded and dead.[24]

Besson makes use of Hollywood's war conventions as well as specific battle scenes from the Joan sub-genre. He also uses a literary-visual quotation in his film: there is a strong resemblance between scenes from the movie and the illustrations of Angela Barthes for Josephine Poole's children's book *Jeanne d'Arc* (Poole, 1998). This is especially true of the scene in which the messenger is revealed to Joan in the open field. The use of already existing images imbues the scenes in the movie with an almost legendary quality – and it is precisely this quality that Besson seeks to destroy in the "perhaps scene" between Joan and the messenger. The intertextual signification system used by Besson suits the unrealistic devices that he delivers in a traditional form. Intertextual relations, however, are also to be found in a film like Fleming's (1948), classified here as a text that works within traditional cinematic historical discourse.

Rémy Pithon's reading of Fleming's film (1985) points to a mode of representation that derives its meaning from cultural influences and prior knowledge of
the cinematic production system. Among the cultural influences, Pithon men-
tions the artificial decor of the ruined Domrémy and its chapel in the opening
scene. This decor is based on an illustration in a well-known nineteenth-century
hagiographic text about Joan, while her armor and particularly her fighting
pose, are based on pre-existent models of heroic paintings. The design of the
court where Fleming's Joan first meets the Dauphin also originates in a nineteenth-century illustration.

The artificial atmosphere generated through these images, however, does not
violate the main goal of the text which is to produce a traditional historical interpretation. Instead, it relies on what are virtually clichés as a form of second-
degree history to reinforce the text's own emphasis on the theme of the occupation of France during World War II. Pithon also discusses the generic conventions of the Hollywood Western and the star system. Fleming's battle scenes are
composed in a manner that evokes the battles of the American Western and the
presence of John Ireland and Ward Bond only reinforces that connection. Gene
Lockhart, who plays the greedy La Tremoille, also played the main role in Fritz
Lang's HANGMEN ALSO DIE (1943), which tells the story of betrayal for profit.
To Pithon's analysis we may add the fact that Ingrid Bergman's Joan in Fleming's film exudes a trail of patriotism borrowed from CASABLANCA (Michael
Curtiz, 1942).

Fleming's JOAN OF ARC relies on visual representation systems that may
evoke the already-known images through the use of familiar locations, faces,
illustrations and conventions. The optional and latent intertextual devices in
Fleming's film testify to the difficulty in telling the Joan story (even using a
traditional approach) without them. His extensive use of this lexicon may explain why Besson made so many references to Fleming's film. Besson, however,
uses manifestly apparent "ready-made" items, including filmic quotations from
the Joan sub-genre. By filming Joan as a fabrication of quotations he is pointing
out the mechanism that produces a "second-degree" past as well as to the existing lexicon.

Turning once more to the alternating images of Joan's face, we can observe a
tradition of self-referential dialogue in the corpus. Renée-Marie Falconetti's face
earned a unique status and has been memorialized in the pantheon of the cinema: shot in close-up in Dreyer's film, her face is full of expression and seems to
be speaking even without words.[25] Nana, the heroine of Godard's VIVRE SA VIE
(1962), goes to the movies and watches the Dreyer film and identifies with the
agonized Joan. Robert Bresson's LE PROCÈS DE JEANNE D'ARC is also a homage
to Dreyer, and Panfilov continues this cinematic palimpsest dialogue by refer-

ring not only to the historical story of Joan of Arc but also to Dreyer's and God-ard's films.

"Historiophoty," as Hayden White (1988: 1193) defined the visual ability of filmic discourse to represent history, becomes "historiography" when cinema uses the photographic image as only one level of discourse in the message it is delivering. Multi-layered cinematic writing, which carries on a dialogue with cinema as well as with other cultural texts, broadens the immediate field of the pictures' significance, infusing them with additional meaning. As the case of Joan teaches us, the repetition of one version after another creates a rupture in the immediate relations between the concreteness of the filmic images and their historical referents. Instead of one history, alternating images suggest various "micro-histories" that engender an intertextual dialogue.[26]

As we shall see in the following chapter, the cinematic institution continues this intertextual dialogue, but in a less explicit manner. Censored drives and unconscious fears that cannot be allowed to appear overtly in the "market of symbolic goods" will be channeled into the game of repetition in various disguises.

Notes

1. See also William Todd Schutz (1999) on Agee and Evans's reportage as autobiography.
2. See André Bazin's famous analysis (1967 [1950, 1955]) in which he admires the use made of deep focus, which enables the viewer to perceive the complexity of reality. Only a later reading of the film might suggest reading it as a meta-historical text (Ivette Biro, private communication, 1986, Linda Hutcheon, 1989).
3. See Brian McHale (1987: 11) on the ontological levels of postmodernist texts.
4. See Hutcheon (1989) and Friedman (1998) for a discussion of the parodic effect of the film, and Anat Zanger (1986) for a discussion of generic procedures in the film.
5. Hayden White (1996: 18) presents a list of imaginary meta-historical texts, beginning with Truman Capote's *In Cold Blood* (1965) and ending with Steven Spielberg's *Schindler's List* (1993). In this respect, the texts of Agee and Wells are even earlier examples of the genre.
6. However, the photographic sign transmits to us several levels of meaning at once: while the accessibility of the photograph makes its seem "natural" for the viewer, it is, in fact, culturally loaded (Barthes, 1977 [1961]).
7. While it is true that every film has within it the simultaneous opposition of presence and absence (as noted by Metz, 1975), in the case of the historical film, this is a reality that disappeared long before the film was shot.
8. The dialogue is based on my notes.
9. The source of Fleming's film is Maxwell Anderson's play, *Joan of Lorraine* (1946).

10. See the observations of Pierre Sorlin (1980), Janet Staiger (1989) and Vivian Sob-chack's (1995 [1990]) on the double exposure of time in the historical film.

11. The American distributors of the film found it too long (Higashi, 1994: 119), and the French distributors did not like the idea of a love story with a soldier "from the other side." They were, after all, in the middle of a war. The love story was cut, the film was reedited, and the shortened version (1917) had, inevitably, a few inexplic-able scenes between Joan and Eric.

12. The original version was burned and the film shown today is a reconstructed ver-sion from 1952 to which a musical soundtrack and short description of Joan's life was added. Dryer based himself on the trial proceedings edited and translated by Pierre Champion (1920).

13. Deborah Linderman has pointed to Dryer's heterogeneous text where "alien materi-al" signifies the impossible position of Joan in patriarchy (1986: 145).

14. Rivette's entire film (1993) is based on testimonies, although there is not one trial scene in the film.

15. We may notice Joan's lips moving, but the voice we hear is a male voice calling: "Joan."

16. Such a presence can also be found in a hagiographic version such as that of Méliès.

17. For a discussion on Besson's film and historical truth, see for example Olivier Bouzy (1999) and Ronald Maxwell (2000).

18. As observed by Carina Yervasi: "The images of Joan of Arc are prolific. One kind of visual reproduction however stands out as the most arresting – this is the cinematic face of Joan of Arc" (1999: 9).

19. None of them, however, has become an automatic reference for Joan's face or a "ci-nematic onomatopoeia," as described by Sobchack (1995 [1990]: 294).

20. On Farrar see also film reviews at *The Bioscope* ("Joan the Woman", January 22, 1920: 47-8) and *Kinematograph Weekly* ("Joan the Woman", January 22, 1920).

21. Historical biography examines the past, writes the past and proposes, like any his-torical text, an interpretation of the past (see Ankersmit, 1994). The historical film, in this sense, can be viewed as a historical, social and cultural document that first and foremost, and wittingly or unwittingly, reveals, as observed by Pierre Sorlin (1980), the individual or collective *mentalité* of its own times.

22. Marina Warner (1979: 275) perceives the relation between text and culture as reflect-ing one another. She presents a typology of the images of Joan under the slogan "a heroine for all seasons," as one image replaces another over the course of history (see Chapter 5 for discussion).

23. For similarities between feminine roles in *Nikita*, *The Fifth Element* and *The Messenger* see Olivier Bouzy (1999: 25).

24. See Régine Pernoud and Marie-Veronique Clin (1998 [1986]: 33-51) for historical re-ferents.

25. See for example the famous article by Béla Balázs on Falconetti's face (1951).

26. See Robert Rosenstone (2000: 184) on the language of visual media, which tends to create multiple, fragmented pasts as micro-histories.

Chapter 7
Disguises

I would like to begin this chapter with a dialogue:

> "Thou hast played boy to every Bulgar in London. Why, even worn men's clothes to please their lust." He stares at her." Answer yea or nay."
>
> "I have worn men's clothes, sir."
>
> "For which thou shalt roast in hell."
>
> "I shan't be alone, sir."
>
> "Did God command you to put on men's clothing?"
>
> "My clothing is a small matter, one of the least. But I did not put on men's clothing by the counsel of any man on earth. I did not put on this clothing, nor do anything else, except at the bidding of God and the angels"
>
> [...]
>
> "When you saw the voice coming to you, was there any light?"
>
> "There was light all about, as there should be! All light does not come to you."
>
> [...]
>
> "Have the saints who appear to you hair?"
>
> "It is a good thing to know."
>
> "What color were his eyes?"
>
> "Dark and quick, not as an honest man's."
>
> "Was he naked?"
>
> "Do you think that God has not wherewithal to clothe him?"

These fragments of dialogue are spoken in the courtroom. The place: England. The interrogator: a man. On the witness stand: a woman. The subject of the cross-examination: a meeting or meetings of the woman with a non- or superhuman entity. Despite the common subject matter and the evident thematic continuity, I must confess that I myself wove these fragments together.[1] In fact, the fragments of the dialogue belong to two separate heroines: to Joan of Arc and her interrogators in 1429 and to Rebecca Lee in 1739, as they appear in the proceedings of the trial recorded in 1996 by Willard Trask in *Joan of Arc: In Her Own Words*, and as described by John Fowles in his 1985 novel *A Maggot*, respectively. My combination of the fragments was made possible by the fact that the interrogation of Joan of Arc hovers in the background of Fowles's novel, which is, in this respect, a rewrite of the original, and can therefore be called a "disguised version."

This chapter will examine the subject of disguised versions, suggesting ways in which their cultural and institutional functions can be understood within that area of "the market of symbolic goods" (Bourdieu's term) hidden from the human eye. Bourdieu's "market" is the mechanism for creating, disseminating and preserving works of art (Bourdieu, 1972). I will use the Joan story and its various cultural transformations in order to clarify the significance of the continual repetition of the same story over and over again for so long a period of time. What are the relations between the "source" (or the original) and a variation? How does one define an "authoritative" or "official" version and what are the limitations of a disguised version? I intend to discuss these questions primarily through the use of three texts: *A Maggot* (John Fowles, 1985), Alien III (David Fincher, 1992) and Breaking the Waves (Lars von Trier, 1996). In what way can one assert that all three constitute versions of a common "source"?[2] Moreover, in what way can we distinguish between "legal" and "illegal" versions in the case of a story that has merited untold versions and adaptations during the 500 years of its existence in the cultural repertory of the West?

In this chapter, I will discuss relations between the source and its unofficial or disguised versions, that is, what I call latent versions. It is my contention that the cultural reworking of the Joan story is, in essence, a process of negotiation intended to legitimize her story and her persona. Within the framework of this process, the source is designated as the desired object,[3] while the desire to find the source and to endow it with historiographic authority is what has engendered the unending chain of versions. As we have seen in the previous chapters, Joan of Arc's historiography reveals the dialectical relations between source and version, when the "source" is nothing but another possible version, and the disguised versions operate according to laws of the "black market." The disguised versions, therefore, function as unofficial agents of the consumers' market, reflecting the consumers' fears and desires.

I   Discourses and Detours

Joan's transgressions against social norms dominate the historiography of this entangled and unceasingly told and retold tale. The attempt to conceal her "sin" is the force that keeps generating endless versions. It is as if one rewrite can take the place of the previous one, as if writing in another code can change or obliterate the significance of the story.

Traditionally, the historiography of Joan of Arc is replete with rhetorical mechanisms aimed at hiding the fact that there is no single, well-defined, authoritative source. The need to legitimate a different version each time stems from the heterogeneous nature of the sources themselves, which creates a kind of *versions-en-abîme* and, consequently, a sense of uncertainty regarding central elements of the myth. The cinematic institution generally complies with cultural regimentation insofar as the Joan story is concerned, but at the same time it has found alternate routes that allow it to include certain additional elements in the telling.

Most of the many cinematic versions of the story continue to spin the tale within the framework of familiar types of discourse. We can point to Méliès's film JOAN OF ARC (1900) or to Cecil B. DeMille's JOAN THE WOMAN (1916) as prototypes of neutral discourse, with a hagiographic or patriotic slant. On the other hand, Otto Preminger's SAINT JOAN (1957) and Werner Herzog and Cheetham's GIOVANNA D'ARCO (1990) employ romantic discourse, giving the myth an additional flavor by treating it clinically, i.e., as romantic-clinical discourse. In these films, Joan/Giovanna is struggling to fulfill herself as a woman although she is also burdened with a deep sense of national responsibility. Her struggle is presented from a psychological angle that recognizes her unorthodox sexuality and labels her as an ominous force.[4] In Herzog and Cheetham's version, based on Verdi's opera (1845, libretto by Solera) Giovanna's inner conflict is depicted as a struggle between two choruses of voices, one of angels and one of demons. When Charles confesses his love to her and tries to convince her to remain with him, angelic voices encourage her to remain faithful to her religious mission and saintly future, while demonic voices urge her to surrender to her passions. Charles, of course, does not hear the voices. But he sees her tortured and distraught visage: "What is she looking at?" he wonders. "What is she pointing at?" The audience hears Giovanna's voices but at the same time sees the scene from Charles's point of view. And so, using combined discourse, Herzog and Cheetham, like Otto Preminger and like Gleb Panfilov (1970) before them, present Joan in the throes of a clinical disputation. Interestingly, she is depicted here as the exemplar of the schizophrenic woman, as conceived by modern psychology (see Friedman and Kaplan, 1967).

The disguised version is another solution that has been adopted by the cinema. Such versions comprise, as we shall see, unofficial readings of the Joan story. The first part of the discussion will deal with the elements necessary to insure that the version – even in disguise – will be recognized as such, that is, as a version. The second part will focus on the disguised versions of the myth in relation to two questions. First, what kind of relations can obtain between the disguised version and the source when the source itself is the desired object?

And, second, in what sense, then, it is possible to relate to the various transformations of the saga as Joan's story?

II   Version and Meta-Version

Shakespeare's version of Joan of Arc, the film version of *King Lear* or, indeed, any witness's testimony about an event, all contain some form of retelling, translation, adaptation, each different in one way or another from the previous narrative text.[5] One can assume that all versions (literary or cinematic), since they belong to the same group or category (versions of "X"), will behave according to the principle of *family resemblance,* as articulated by Wittgenstein.[6]

Applying this principle to either declared or disguised versions of "X" requires that we uncover certain elements germane to the "X" series in order that we may understand and properly analyze the version. On the other hand, the identification of these immutable or variable elements – which one can expect to find in any version of "X" *a priori* – can never be fully exhaustive. There will always be hidden parameters that can be identified only *a posteriori.* Disguised versions – and such is the case with Joan of Arc – emphasize precisely those parameters that declared versions seek to conceal.

As a category, the "X" series of versions functions in relation to both members of its own series and members of other series. To explicate this issue let us take the form of the letter "a": "a" relates at one and the same time to other forms (fonts) of the same letter (e.g., "a" or "A"), from which it differs. At the same time it conducts a dialogue, carried on along the axis of difference and repetition with other letters. Versions of the same series relate to each other in the same way as do various forms of the letter "A". In every group of versions, as testified to by the various forms of the letters, there exists a dynamic among the members (see table 1).[7]

If all the letters "A" in the table represent versions of Joan of Arc, each of the other letters of the alphabet will represent other categories of versions of, say, *Hamlet* or *Cinderella.* Nevertheless, versions can belongs to a variety of sub-categories while sharing common traits with other sub-categories (e.g., aesthetic or cultural).

With the aid of this illustration we can see that in every repetition there is a difference in relation to another text or other texts belonging to the same series. For, as Deleuze says, the repetition occurs where there is no absolute identity although there is more than mere resemblance (1994 [1969]). As an intertextual activity, the repetition, in the form of another version, maintains dialectical relations with the original. Are these necessarily derivative relations and, if so, in what respect?

	A	B	C	D	E	F	G
1	Balmoral	Cardinal	Squire	Glastonbury	Arnold Böcklin	Bottleneck	Countdown
2	Eckmann Schrift	Futura Black	Hobo	Lazybones	Old English	Revue	Park Avenue
3	Romic Bold	Tintoretto	Vivaldi	Univers 67	Airkraft	Apollo	Algerian
4	Astra	Baby Teeth	Block Up	Bombere	Buster	Calypso	Columbian Italic
5	Aristocrat	Company	Glaser Stencil	Cathedral	Good Vibrations	Le Golf	Harrington
6	Harlow Solid	Motter Ombra	Masquerade	Phyllis	Pluto Outline	Process	Primitive
7	Magnificat	Quicksilver	Raphael	Roco	Shatter	Stripes	Sinaloa
8	Stop	Stack	Piccadilly	Neptun	Motter Tektura	Odin	Yagi Link Double

Table 2: Various Fonts of the Letter A (Hofstadter, 1985 [1982], p. 243)

There are two major criteria that are relevant in examining relations between original and version: a referential and a textual presence. First, with respect to the referential level: the relation can be declared or latent. The title, for example, can either declare its connection to a category of versions or divert attention from it. On the textual level there can be different degrees of presence, ranging from the local to the global. As I will try to show below, types of intertextual relations stem from interactions between the referential and the textual.[8]

Type of Intertextual Relations	Type of Referential Level	Textual Level
quotation	declared reference	local presence
direct allusion	explicit	local presence
indirect allusion	implicit	local presence
- - - - - - - - - - - - - - - - - -mise-en-abime- -[9]		
parody	implicit/declared reference in the title (optional) or by generic affiliation (optional)	global presence through local signifiers scattered (thematic/stylistic)
transformation (adaptation)	" "	" "
imitation	" "	" "

Table 3: Intertextual Relations

A version, like an imitation or an adaptation, belongs essentially to the domain of "hypertextuality" (in Genette's terminology), which occurs when a later text (a hypertext) is derived from an earlier text (the hypotext) (Genette, 1982: 11-4). Hypertextuality is not local in scope but present throughout the entire text. While a declared version can signify its connection to the original story through its title, both declared and disguised versions can do this by repeating certain central elements throughout, or by including "clusters of significant signals"[10] or by *mise-en-abîme*.[11] In any case, creating a version or an imitation requires the duplication of certain formulas: the "source" has to run through the new version. In the words of Ben-Porat (1983), cultural imitation is an individual *parole*, in a specific historical and cultural context, and based on the *langue* of the original. If we apply this contention to the narrative grammar of the version, we can say that the specific expression of a version is a manifestation of the *langue*. But protruding from the manifestation is the implicit syntagmatic axis of actions and agents of action from the source, carrying on a dialogue with the actual actions and agents of action of the version. Or, as Greimas (1977 [1969]) calls it, the surface structure. The manifestations of a specific version and the manner in which they are interwoven with the implicit surface structure are the elements that constitute the deep structure of the text, that paradigmatic "massing of forces" that constructs the point of view of the text. Despite the possibility of variegated manifestations, every version can create a deep structure that echoes that of the original.[12]

One of the central functions of the imitation, like that of the version, is to position itself vis-à-vis the original in a relevant contemporary context (see Ben-Porat, 1983). In this sense, the literary and cinematic versions of Joan of Arc constitute a unique case insofar as they relate to the "historical source." As I noted above, the genealogy of the chain of versions of the Joan story maintains relations of desire with the "source" – in itself a multiplicity of versions.[13] On other hand, the veil of censorship that enshrouds official versions dictates the manner in which the story will be told. Thus, all official versions seek to present themselves as the "ultimate truth," to the exclusion of all others. At the same time, all the disguised versions seek to present the traumatic elements of the story. This is the "social narrative" about an extraordinary female who transgresses against one of society's central taboos and is punished for it. The disguised (unofficial) versions deal with these traumatic elements by rewriting them palimpsestically, thus conducting a (forbidden) dialogue with the Joan myth.

III   Disguised Versions

Looking at the Joan corpus, we may conclude that the aesthetics of the version is based upon a maneuvering between immutable and variable elements. This dialectic is especially visible with regard to three core elements: the voices, her dress, and the trial. These are the components that appear again and again and that, in retrospect, disclose the "contours" of the meta-version.

The voices are extremely significant and yet unusually enigmatic in Joan's career. As we have noted, they were the key to the support given to her by her family, by the commander at Voucauleurs, by the Dauphin Charles, by the religious establishment in Poitiers, by her captors at Rouen, and by the judges at her trials. And they were of primary importance in the process of her canonization by the pope.[14] So it is not surprising that the voices are a constant element in so many versions. The female element in her identity is central to Joan's story and the components of her identity are her dress and her voices. One is the signifier of her self-fulfillment, the other is the signified. While independence, self-expression and public activity were outside the pale for women, Joan uses the voices as a possible channel for achieving involvement. Joan's sin is violating

the taboo: she declares – through her voices and her dress – that she has a right
to engage in men's affairs (Warner, 1979). Even if the encyclopedic reservoir
attempts to minimize these problematic areas, they are, nevertheless, visible between the lines and in the language of the indictment: no less than twelve
charges deal with the fact that she wore men's attire. As Warner points out
(ibid.): through her dress Joan obtained rights reserved for men. At the same
time, without pretending that she is anything but a young maid, she under-
mined accepted sexual distinctions in order to create "a third order," on the
lines of the angels she so loved.

Even if *A Maggot* (Fowles, 1985), ALIEN III (Fincher, 1992) and BREAKING THE
WAVES (Von Trier, 1996) do not "declare" (through their titles) their connection
to Joan of Arc, the three major elements – voices, dress and trials – appear in all
three. That is to say, that while the referential levels of the three do not declare
any connection to Joan of Arc, the textual levels reveal a similar surface structure. It would seem that there is no connection between the ways the three plots
manifest themselves. Yet on closer examination, we can see the same implicit
syntagmatic axis conducting a dialogue with the Joan story through the surface
structure. The rhetorical devices used by these versions all operate as part of the
double referential mechanism – a term coined by Hrushovsky (1982):[15]

> By saying that a literary text creates an Internal Field of Reference (IFR), I do not
> imply any absolute separation of a "fictional world" from reality. Indeed, the reader
> of a work of fiction must "imagine" an "intentional" field or "imaginary space" into
> which he projects the reconstructed characters, events, meanings. At the same time,
> however, semantic material within a literary text may refer or relate to External Fields
> of Reference [ExFR] (1982: 75).

With regard to the three texts under discussion, and to the entire Joan corpus,
the distinction between the internal and external fields of reference is vital. On
the one hand, the significant elements are located on the diegetic axis of the plot
(= the internal referent). On the other, the very same elements function as signals pointing to a reality external to the text, one that exists in the twilight area
between reality and imagination. This reality is mediated by an untold number
of earlier cultural works and historical texts whose original has been lost or,
perhaps, never even existed (= the external referent). The external field of reference here has been created by more than five centuries of tradition and thus
contains vital elements from the historiography of Joan of Arc as they have
been incorporated into Western culture.

In order to illustrate this point, I will discuss the subject of "voices." This significant signal appears in BREAKING THE WAVES primarily through the heroine's
conversations with God. At the beginning of the film Beth declares that "it is
silly that only men can express opinions in church," and she is upset because

there are no church bells. She conducts a series of conversations with a non-presence whose answers she herself provides, albeit in a somewhat thickened voice. Her conversations refer to a previous event in the film in which she asks God to bring home her new husband, Jan, who is working at a distant oil rig. But the referential mechanism is also aimed at a reality external to the text. As in Herzog and Cheetham's GIOVANNA D'ARCO (1990) for example, two separate voices run simultaneously through Beth's mind. [16] The clinical model of the schizophrenic hovers in the air and is associated with the different order of things proposed by the heroine. Beth has asked God to send Jan home. The voice asks: "Are you sure that is what you want?" Beth answers: "Yes, I am sure." Immediately following this, Jan returns home seriously injured in the wake of an accident at the rig.

> The voice: "I had to test you. Your love for Jan was being tested."
> Beth: "Thank you for not letting him die."

At first Beth is encouraged by these conversations. She believes that she will be able to save Jan despite the grim medical report. Later, when she is on the verge of despair, Beth is unable to make contact with her voices. Like Joan in her prison cell, she tries. "What is happening?" she asks. "Father, where are you?" But there is no response. Only towards the end of the film, with the distant pealing of church bells,[17] do her voices return to her. They encourage her in her last attempt to sacrifice herself for Jan's recovery, by submitting to sexual relations with brutal sailors. Beth is now dressed as a whore:

> Beth: "Father, why are you not with me now?"
> The voice: "I am with you, what do you want?"
> Beth: "Where have you been?"
> The voice: "What did you think, that there were no other people who wanted to talk to me?"
> Beth: "Of course I didn't think about it, but now, are you with me?"
> The voice: "Of course I am with you, Beth. You know that."

We have here not only the schizophrenic model of the voices, and not only the connection between the church bells and the voices. We also have society's opposition to Beth's attempt to create a different sexual and social order. The attempt to control Beth's sexuality is made by her close family (with the exception of Jan), the medical establishment, the priest and officials of the municipality. As in the story of Joan of Arc, here too we have the figures of the benevolent priest and the even more benevolent doctor. Dr. Richardson tries to convince Beth to give up her struggle by bringing her a letter signed by Jan just as Joan's inquisitors bring her a letter allegedly signed by the Dauphin Charles. Here too we have an excommunication trial conducted by the church during her lifetime and another trial after her death. Like Joan, Beth, in her distress, begins to doubt the validity of her struggle. Perhaps, when all is said and done, she was mistaken. She is on the verge of death and realizes that Jan's condition is still precarious. The narrative is resolved with Jan's recovery, testifying to the fact that Beth's order has prevailed over that of the respected scientific establishment.

The heroine of ALIEN III, Ripley, is the sole survivor of an alien attack that lands on a closely guarded prison installation, Fiorina 181. She gains the ear of the installation's physician who is ready to hear her out, albeit with reservations, but antagonizes the commander when she tries to explain the reason for the distressing situation that has overtaken the installation. Like Joan, Ripley's "encounters of the third kind" (with an angel in one case, an alien in the other) provide her with special knowledge. As a result "voices" from another world echo in her mind. Interestingly, society reacts to the voices in both places in a similar manner. The viewer, equipped with extra-textual knowledge (the first two parts of the series), tends to side with the heroine's inner truth. Ripley is aware of the fact that although she took all possible precautions when she was commander of the spaceship (at the end of ALIEN II), the indestructible alien has penetrated the isolated prison installation along with her, and the victims are piling up. The commander believes that Ripley's female presence simply upped the level of violence among the prisoners. When she tries to talk to him he assures her that he doesn't care for her opinion because she is not familiar with all the facts. Only when he finishes work will he be happy to "chat with her." The conversation takes place in the office of the commander, which has a barred window. Ripley, in men's clothes, her head shaven (like Joan's in many prison scenes), confronts the commander and one of his assistants who give no credence to her opinions:

> The commander: "If I understood you rightly, Lieutenant, it is a creature about a meter and a half high, with acid rather than blood in its veins. It arrived together with you in the spaceship, it kills indiscriminately and, in general, is not very nice. And you expect me to believe this on your say-so?"
> Ripley: "I don't expect anything."
> The commander's assistant: "That's some story, a real fairytale."
> The commander: "What do you suggest that we do?"
> Ripley: "Are you armed?"

Like Joan before her, Ripley tries to convince the commander to prepare for an offensive, but the commander, like Joan's interrogators when her answers do not suit their expectations, decides to imprison her (in the installation's infirmary). After the alien adds more victims to his list, Ripley, terrified, runs to the commander who has not yet heard about the latest victim – the installation's doctor. He tries to provide his own explanation for the previous victims. Ripley cuts him short with: "It's here. It trapped Clemens in the infirmary!!" To which the commander responds: "Take this madwoman to the infirmary." Before he has finished the sentence the alien surprises him, grabs him from behind, raises him up and does away with him. There is a parallel here with the soldier in the battlefield who tries to undermine Joan's authority and dies on the spot.[18] This is justice from heaven, and is therefore unassailable vindication. As in the Joan story and in BREAKING THE WAVES, Ripley is vindicated only after her death, when the story is resolved by the testimony of three survivors.

Like Joan, Ripley shaves her head and like Joan, she is interrogated over and over again about the truth of her story. And like Joan she continues to fight for what she believes to be right. She tries to convince the doctor, the commander; the prisoners. When representatives of the company arrive at the installation, the extent of their betrayal becomes evident: they have not come to rescue Ripley and the prisoners, and they are interested only in saving the alien in order to further their plans for the development of lethal weapons. Like Joan, Ripley faces a difficult decision: to abandon her truth or die. And like Joan, she negotiates with her captors the terms of her surrender. When she realizes that she cannot trust them, she chooses self-immolation. The narrative grammar of the surface structure of ALIEN III, like those of the Joan saga and BREAKING THE WAVES, includes a wide range of elements. There are: voices, the mission, the obstacles on the way to achievement, a change of dress, shaving the head (optional), success, interrogation, betrayal, death by fire and recognition (limited) after death.[19] (For Joan's trial in Fleming's *Joan of Arc* and Ripley's trial in Fincher's *Alien III* see ill. VII a and VII b)

The connection between *A Maggot* and the Joan story is more abstract and not all the elements of the narrative grammar appear. Nevertheless, *A Maggot* contributes a new factor to the deep structure of the Joan story, something that we can call meta-textual understanding. Fowles uncovers the convention that structures the historical novel in general and the Joan story as a whole. It is the ontological tension that exists by virtue of the double status of the components both in the text's internal field of reference and in the information afforded by external fields of reference. Ann Lee, a historical figure, was an English textile worker who considered herself the female counterpart of Jesus. She emigrated to America in 1774 in order to escape religious persecution and was among the founders of the Shaker movement in the United States. Her followers called her Mother Ann. *A Maggot* is a fictional work that borrows the conventions of non-fiction in order to recreate the few months in 1736 before her birth. The novel deals with an unexplained and sinister occurrence concerning the disappearance of a young nobleman in what was taken to be the work of the devil (or, perhaps, aliens). These events were indirectly responsible, according to Fowles, for the birth of Ann Lee. Constructed in the form of depositions given to an investigator by all the protagonists, from the prostitute Rebecca Lee, Ann Lee's mother, to the malicious actor/servant, David Jones, the novel combines the investigations with facsimile reproductions of a contemporary newspaper, *Historical Chronicle*, printed sporadically throughout the text.

Fowles introduces minutes of the proceedings of certain trials in order to point out "encounters of the third kind" that had taken place contrary to the known chronology of the heroine's life.[20] As Fowles notes in the epilogue of *A Maggot*:

> Readers who know something of what that Manchester baby was to become in the
> real world will not need telling how little this is a historical novel. I believe her actual
> birth was two months before my story begins, on 29 February 1736. I know nothing in
> reality of her mother, and next to nothing of various other characters. It may be that
> books and documents exist that might have told me more of them in historical terms
> than the little I know: I have consulted none. I repeat, this is a maggot, not an attempt,
> either in fact or in language, to reproduce known history (1985: 455).

Fowles declares that he is not writing history, but a maggot – that is, something like the wispy remains of an old tune. Like ALIEN III and BREAKING THE WAVES, *A Maggot* revolves around a young women struggling for her "truth" against a society that wishes to control her sexuality. In this way, unofficial or "black" versions that refrain from declaring their kinship with the family of Joan versions are, nevertheless, revealed by their look-alike surface structures. The aesthetics of repetition produces, in this case, two parallel processes. On the one hand, the presence in disguised versions of significant signals – like voices – testifies to the transformation's kinship with the family. Like DNA, the signals break through the disguise. On the other hand, the projection of a different manifestation on similar surfaces points to the skeletons in this family's closet.

IV   Repetition, Cultural Memory and Trauma

Repetition is, first and foremost, a movement in time. According to Kierkegaard, the act of repeating is itself intervention in the movement of time. It is a caesura, the pause that defines what was and prepares us for what will come.[21] The urge for repetition, however, as observed by Sigmund Freud (1955 [1920]), stems from the need to control a traumatic experience. And Harold Bloom adds:

> The compulsion here remains that of repetition, but with a reversal of *unconscious*
> meaning. In the Isolation of an idea from its original emotional investment, repetition
> also remains dominant (1977 [1973]: 81).

The fact that Western culture returns again and again to the same story testifies to the fact that the conflict between the social order and Joan's challenge to it has not yet been resolved. Thus, despite Joan's official canonization (in 1920), night after night, at movie houses and theaters all over the world, she is still being burned alive. In this respect, the disguised versions allow themselves to go one step further. By not declaring their referential field, they remain unfettered by the social censorship that has been imposed on official versions for so many generations. Stripped of the desire for that mythical "source," the three disguised "Joans" – Beth, Ripley and Rebecca Lee – present a threat to the established order because through the narrative disguise one can also catch glimpses of what has been suppressed. As noted by Gilles Deleuze:

> Repetition is constituted only with and through the *disguises* which affect the terms and relations of the real series, but it is so because it depends upon the virtual object as an immanent instance which operates above all by displacement. (1994 [1969]): 105, my emphasis).

Compulsive repetition, disguise, imitation – these are what nurture the "black-market" versions. In the case of Joan of Arc, the cultural censorship imposed on the manner in which it is permitted to tell the story also gives these black-market versions their freedom. By means of disguise these versions mask their family resemblance to the series. On the other hand, the disguise enables them to "smuggle in" censored signals that relate to the source and undermine its authority. In this way, the link between the source, knowledge and sexual identity is re-examined openly, thus redefining the entire series.

Notes

1. The following are the sources:
    "Thou hast played boy to every Bulgar in London. Why, even worn men's clothes to please their lust." He stares at her. "Answer yea or nay."
    "I have worn men's clothes, sir."
    For which thou shalt roast in hell."
    "I shan't be alone, sir."
    − − − *A Maggot* John Fowles, 1985: 48.
    "Did God command you to put on men's clothing?"
    "My clothing is a small matter, one of the least. But I did not put on men's clothing by the counsel of any man on earth. I did not put on this clothing, nor do anything else, except at the bidding of God and the angels" […].
    "When you saw the voice coming to you, was there any light?"
    "There was light all about, a so there should be! All light does not come to you" […].
    "Have the saints who appear to you hair?"

"It is a good thing to know."
——— *In Her Own Words*, 1996 (1841-49): 100, 103.
"What color were his eyes?"
"Dark and quick, not as an honest man's."
"Was he naked?"
——— *A Maggot* 1985: 69
"Do you think that God has not wherewithal to clothe him?"
——— *In Her Own Words,* 1996: 105

2.   Brian McHale suggested the resemblance between *A Maggot* and Joan of Arc to me in a private communication.

3.   See Lacan's distinctions on this subject and his attitude to the concept of "real." In many ways, the desire for the "source" is a desire for the inaccessible "real" (Lacan, 1977, and Lacan 1982 [1966]).

4.   This short overview does not permit me to mention the whole range of versions. For a more elaborate discussion, see Chapter 5.

5.   See Barbara Hernstein-Smith (1980).

6.   Wittgenstein (1958), as noted, emphasized that while members of the same family can resemble one another in different ways, they do not necessarily share a unique collection of common traits. For a detailed discussion see Chapter 2.

7.   See also the discussion in chapter one, page 38.

8.   I am indebted for this table to an article by Lucien Dällenbach (1976).

9.   The *mise-en-abîme*, despite its local presence, illuminates the entire text. In this respect, it is in a transitional position between local and global. For a discussion of the *mise-en-abîme* see McHale (1985) and Dällenbach (1989).

10.   What Peter Donaldson calls "salient sequences" (1996).

11.   See in this context Michal R. Friedman on *mise-en-abîme* in film (1996).

12.   As discerned by Claude Lévi-Strauss (1979 [1958]). A version can create a deep structure that counters or dismantles the deep structure of the original and, in this way, expresses its position as regards the original.

13.   Most of the versions claim to accurately reconstruct the historical period during which Joan was active and this is the source of their authoritative tone. On the other hand, the necessity of updating the versions of cinematic texts is even more imperative because of the concrete dimension of its analogical signifiers, when compared with the abstract dimension of symbolic signifiers in the literary text.

14.   A detailed discussion of Joan's voices in the sources and versions is presented in Chapters 5 and 6.

15.   A term I have introduced in the context of cinematic biography (Chapter 6).

16.   See also Herzog's version in the previous chapter.

17.   Thus Otto Preminger's Joan says to Dunois: "Let me tell you a secret. Here, from the bells, I hear the voices."

18.   See e.g., Fleming's narrative structure (1948).

19.   Kathleen Murphy (1992) notes that the link between Dreyer's film *The Trial of Joan of Arc* and Fincher's *Alien III* is based on the fact that they both shave their heads. It is my contention that the link between Fincher's film and the Joan saga is based on significant signals scattered throughout the text as a whole.

20. In this context it is relevant to mention Brian McHale's insight that postmodernist texts tend to foreground ontological issues that raise questions about the "world" of the text (1987: 7-11).
21. See Arne Melberg, 1990.

Conclusion

Chapter 8
Repetitions as Hidden Streams

> Only the mutations of the strong survive. The weak, the anonymous, the
> defeated leave few marks [...] history loves only those who dominate her: it
> is a relationship of mutual enslavement.
> Salman Rushdie (*Shame*)

The various stories, myths and icons we have examined here have been inscribed in a number of chains of repetition. Some of them are interchangeable,
like those of Marion and Susanna, Olympia and Carmen, or Joan of Arc, Beth,
Ripley, Rebecca and Ann-Lee. The many versions that constitute these chains
are characterized by their palimpsestic relationships both with their source or
sources, and among themselves. Furthermore, the long tradition of these chains,
which sometimes, as in the case of Joan of Arc, have roots in the Middle Ages,
has endowed them with the status of a myth. The train of versions in the wake
of the tale generates the charm of the déjà vu and obfuscates the distinction
between source and version.

My discussion of the chains of *Psycho, Carmen* and *Joan* has been framed by
two sets of questions. The first has to do with the act of repetition itself: What
are the relations that exist, potentially, between "source" and version, as well as
among the versions themselves? The second has to do with the specific text
being repeated. What is the significance of the re-articulation of the same old
story over and over again? These questions have, in the course of time, elicited
different answers within the context of changing aesthetic and cultural norms.
However, as we may conclude by now, these two aspects of repetition are inter-
twined. In this context I would like to identify here the *karaoke* spectacle as a
metonym for a ritual in which – following Roman Jakobson's model of communication (1960) – both addresser and addressee are involved. Like the karaoke,
successive versions involve a chain of performative acts. Each spectacle of karaoke suggests the rewriting of an already known "melody" while addresser and
addressee replace each other. We may ask then, what is it that seduces both
performers and audiences to consume more of the same specific melody?

Throughout the present book, we have looked at the re-significations of each
chain from various perspectives: original and copy, constants and variables,
manifest and latent, pleasure and *jouissance*. The textual economy and the inter-

textual relations of the various versions have been read as "fingerprints" of the cinematic institution in its relationship with other cultural, social and aesthetic systems. These fingerprints reflect the cinematic institution's system of preferences, aimed at habituating the viewer to certain modes of spectatorship.

Cinematic repetitions can be identified as components of the cinematic institution that maintains the medium as a socio-cultural activity. As a "mental machinery" which internalizes norms of spectatorship (Metz, 1975), the cinematic institution mediates between social structure and the subject in order to construct the collective subconscious according to prevailing schemes of society. In this sense, the cinematic versions of *Psycho*, *Carmen* and *Joan of Arc* that have regularly appeared throughout the 20th century, from the inception of cinema to the present day, not only reflect cultural needs but also direct them. Furthermore, the presence of these stories outside of the familiar schemes of genre, *auteurs*, stars or national cinema, suggests their existence as hidden streams in the ongoing flow of films.

My discussion in the preceding chapters focused upon the different trajectories plotted by three of the most widespread cinematic repetitions: the corpora of *Psycho*, *Carmen* and *Joan of Arc*. I would like to conclude the discussion by exploring some of the common features of all the three corpora. The reading of the three chains of variation in this book has been done, mainly, vertically, that is, among the various members of the same group. I would now like to introduce an additional perspective, a horizontal one, which will compare in brief these chains of repetition one against the other.

I   Looking Back

PSYCHO – and its remakes, "prequels" and sequels – has become a fetish in a culture in which the myth of *Orpheus and Eurydice* and *Susanna and the Elders* also have pride of place. Interestingly, *Susanna and the Elders* is inscribed in PSYCHO in a painting which conceals the hole through which Norman will peep at Marion as she bathes. The defining element of these stories (and of many others) is the male gaze, a gaze that will produce the woman as the passive victim of a male fantasy. By recognizing the *Susanna and the Elders* painting as the paradigm of the voyeuristic tradition that firmly establishes a binary opposition between female passivity and male activity, we can identify the various versions of PSYCHO as part of this chain.

Within the cultural context of this tradition, we may posit Manet's *Olympia* (1865) as a "reverse shot" of *Susanna and the Elders*. Functioning both within and outside of the visual regime, it challenges borders and, simultaneously, signals obedience and disobedience (see Clark, 1980, and Wollen, 1980). *Olympia* might be perceived as depicting the classical mode of representation pointing towards its own functioning. Paradoxically, only when viewers identify the place of the subject do the codes that led them to occupy this place become visible to them.

My reading of *Olympia* emphasizes its significance in the cultural and aesthetic atmosphere of the late 19th and the entire 20th century. *Olympia* apparently crosses the boundaries between the sacred and the profane – hence, its followers must attempt to reconstitute these boundaries once again. *Olympia* seems to be the most subversive text of all, at least from our limited early-21st-century perspective. In 1983 Rutault exhibited his work *Michael Delluc, 10 Avril 1983, 10 rue de Belzunce, Paris 10* (1983), in which Delluc's pose and gesture paraphrase that of Olympia (and do so twice – once with Delluc wearing clothing and once in the nude). The photographic texts ironically invert the rules of the game by locating a naked man at the mercy of the viewer's gaze, and thus underscores the extent to which *Olympia* has become part of our cultural and aesthetic repertoire in the more than one hundred years since the painting was first shown. By the same logic, the figure of Carmen was replaced with that of a male dancer (Baryshnikov), as it is in Roland Petit's ballet *Carmen* (France, 1980).

Pointing to places of disturbance, chains like that of *Olympia* might be used to trace cultural *doxa* and social taboos as well as aesthetic traditions, including the act of repetition itself. Manet's metonymical transformation of Giorgeone's painting lays bare the pleasure of spectatorship and, at the same time, generates another chain, the chain of *Olympia*. Looking at the two chains, Susanna's *Psycho* chain consists of only metaphorical relations with its source and members, whereas the *Venus/Olympia/Carmen* chain has both metaphorical and metonymical relations. Theoretically, of course, any chain, including the *Psycho* chain, may change course.

The desire to have the already-known experience repeated is accompanied by the presentiment that it never will be. The subject-viewer oscillates between the initial experience of pleasure, the traces left by this experience and future attempts to repeat it. Pleasure is located in the moment of homeostasis between tension and release, that is, when difference and repetition are in equilibrium. *Jouissance*, in contrast, relates to the freezing of the moment of the annihilation of tension, that is, when differences and repetition are not satisfactorily balanced (see Barthes, 1977 and Paul Willemen 1975, cited in Steve Neale, 1980: 48). In this sense, we may identify Van Sant's PSYCHO as the ultimate actualization of pleasure, that is, originality as repetition.[1] Manet's *Olympia*, on the other hand, by refusing to position the figure of the woman within the conventions of "to-be-looked-at-ness," brings to crisis the very experience of spectatorship and produces a state of loss: the viewer finds that traditional pleasure has been destroyed and *jouissance* suggested instead.

These two sets of concepts, metaphor/metonymy and pleasure/*jouissance*, share some similarities with respect to the relationship between a version and its source. One type of version – the metaphorical transformation – satisfies its spectators through reinforcing the affinity between the source and the version, thus functioning as cultural affirmation. The other kind – the metonymical transformation – creates a rupture between itself and the existing cultural tradition. The spectator experiences frustration as the presentiment that there will be no return to the initial experience is fulfilled. If, following Lévi-Strauss (1972) and Thomas Pavel (1981), we distinguish between the sacred and the profane components of a myth, the sacred element must remain untouched. Otherwise *jouissance* results and pleasure is denied. In this way we may understand the struggle to survive of both *Carmen* and *Joan*, two chains that I locate in the imaginary archive of the cinema along with *Olympia*. Like *Olympia* the stories of *Carmen* and *Joan*, with their genetic seal of social transgression, encapsulate the threat to destroy traditional pleasure.

II   Repetitions and Variations

As observed by Noël Carroll:

> If the institutional theory claims a certain type of complexity as the determinant feature of film, then the final, though most crucial, portion of the theory involves a review of the processes of articulation as examples of complex elements that cannot only repeat but amplify and repudiate earlier uses of those elements (Carroll, 1996: 385).

In this context, I have examined the phenomenon of repetitions and variations of the same stories. Working within the framework of the institutional approach enables us to understand the histories of chains of versions as a responsive element within a hierarchical structure, and to demonstrate how the cinematic institution maintains a mutual relationship with the cultural system at large.[2] Thus, to delineate the histories of *Psycho*, *Carmen* and *Joan of Arc* as series of re-articulations and re-significations, means to spotlight the question of how aesthetics and cultural norms function in given times and circumstances, rather than how aesthetics and cultural norms function in principle.[3] Three sets of oppositions constitute the necessary components that reflect this interactive "poly-system" (Even-Zohar, 1990): (a) dynamic versus static (or variable versus constant), (b) center versus periphery (or canonic versus non-canonic), and (c) dia-chronic versus synchronic.

The instability of the *Carmen* corpus is already inherent in its dual source, as well as in the structure of opera as a collage of clichés. The phenomenon of *versionality-en-abîme* of the *Joan of Arc* corpus shapes its perpetual legitimacy, while *Olympia* – a version preceded by two sources – turns into a source in its own right. Source and version may be perceived as a distinctive dichotomy con-sisting of derivative relationships. On the other hand, the source rearticulates itself constantly vis-à-vis its versions. Thus, Saura and Paco de Lucia's flamenco rhythm in *Carmen* becomes the dance equivalent of Bizet's opera, Bizet's opera is represented in Godard's version via a casual tune whistled in a bar, and *Car-men* as a popular concept may come to function as the name of a computer game entitled *Carmen San Diego* (USA, 1991).[4]

In this sense, each new version will redefine the source, and by the same lo-gic, there can be no possible definition of source that includes all possible varia-tions. No "meta-version" exists, much as no "meta-font" can exist *a priori* (see Hofstadter 1985: 283). In this context, it is possible to identify *Olympia* as a painted version of *Carmen*, especially of the *Habañera*. Do both gestures not in-scribe within themselves the feminine declaration of simultaneous obedience and disobedience? The study of source–version relationships is a clear example of this elusive phenomenon, since the object of study changes under observa-tion. Thus, like the manuscript in Umberto Eco's *The Name of the Rose*, the source we are looking for is only a reproduction or a revised edition – that is, a con-struct of contemporary readings of its versions.

The cinematic chain of versions spanning the 20th century suggests that the *Carmen* corpus is a sensitive seismograph that reflects aesthetic and technical changes. However, Carmen, as a subaltern by gender, ethnicity and class has to be re-inscribed in a subject-position different from that of Don José. Formulated already in Mérimée and Bizet, this principle is repeated "inaccurately" to use Butler's term (1993), in films under specific social restrictions, prohibitions and taboos in a ritual that both examines and constitutes the norms. The traveller's gaze, the "pseudo-objective discourse," the indirect and partial representations by stereotypes, the simultaneous fear of and fascination with the "other" and the denial – all aim to produce pleasure in this ritual of *Carmen* repetitions. Dri-ven by a fantasy of control, the repeated portrayal of Carmen and the gypsies on the screen has at least three "master knobs" (Hofstadter's term, 1985 [1982]): first, the *Habañera*, Carmen's voice; second, the alternating ethnic identities of Carmen and the gypsies; and third, the smuggling gesture. As to the first, Car-men's voice, from the silent movies (DeMille, Chaplin), through the talkies (Re-iniger, Amadori, Christian-Jaque), and down to a number of postmodernist ver-sions (Saura, Godard and Brook), Carmen's song has been "rewritten," manipulated, and gradually muted. As for the second, the carnival of masks that indicate changes from the Roma minority to black, white or Asian suggest a shift in the center/periphery dynamic. This fluidity of ethnic identities functions as a "projective identification" (Mathijs van de Port's term; in Iordanova, 2001: 214) in a way that enables us to redefine and control the border between white and colored people. And the third, the production of a dialectic movement between legal and illegal space in various versions enables us to portray Carmen as a woman who acts outside the law and, in this way, to question her legitimacy.

The wall and the guarded gate exist in order to separate the civilized and structured white world from the nomadic life and open spaces of the Romani people. In this sense the "gesture of smuggling" seems to function as a pocket of resistance to hegemony. However, by including the smuggling gesture as well as the punishment of those involved in the act in the diegesis, the cinematic corpus reassures viewers that the existing social order will be maintained.

Interestingly, the four versions produced between 1983-84 suggest a salient synchronic axis in addition to the diachronic axes of successive versions created over the course of cinema history: Godard's PRÉNOM CARMEN (1983), Saura's CARMEN (1983), Brook's TRAGEDY OF CARMEN (1984) and Rosi's CARMEN (1984). The coexistence of these four versions should theoretically constitute the perfect example for any evolutionary model. Alas, the four 1983-84 *Carmen* versions refuse to comply. Godard's, Saura's and Brook's versions are all meta-diegetic versions that deconstruct the totality of the myth through ontological tension. This tendency finds its almost utopian declaration in Brook's three successive versions of CARMEN (1984), and simultaneously its (dystopian) anticlimax in Rosi's CARMEN (1984). On the other hand, all these versions, each in its own way, continue the tradition of depriving Carmen of her credo and of questioning her legitimacy.

The reading of the cinematic versions of *Joan of Arc* follows the three central elements of the myth of *Joan* itself: the inseparable images of her voices, her dress as a key to her problematic femininity and the trial as the manifest standpoint of a given version. These three elements, which recur in each version, constitute the evaluative mechanism of the versions as well as of the cultural narrative of Joan of Arc, which has almost no other stable entities.

Although historical and cultural discourse tries to censor the real drama behind rhetorical curtains, this drama is visible in the inner logic of the story. Its epicenter is the problematic androgyny – not only sexual, but also social – of Joan of Arc. Her voices and her mode of dress are the two inseparable elements of her self-fulfillment. As observed by Warner, prophecy was a legitimate vocation for women at a time when any other career was forbidden: "Women used prophecy because so few other means of expression were available to them" (Warner 1979: 85).

The multiplicity of historical "sources," as well as Joan's problematic sexuality, has produced a rather rigid tradition on how to tell the story while remaining within the confines of propriety. A repertoire of "ready-made" narrative schemes and discourses dominate the regimentation of the *Joan* story and control its transmission: hagiographic and patriotic attributions, on the one hand, and romantic-clinical, on the other.

It is worth mentioning here an early example, a 1900 film directed by Georges Méliès. The fantastic aspect of Méliès's text reveals itself through the animation techniques of its writing as well as through the revelation scenes, the miraculous punishment of the sinner and Joan's reception in heaven. While the film structure of twelve tableaux alludes to Christ's Via Dolorosa, the design of the protagonist alludes to another familiar text. In Méliès's animated drawings Joan is a tall, thin girl with very long, curly hair, who bears a remarkable resemblance to Alice in John Tenniel's illustrations for Lewis Carroll's *Alice in Wonderland* (1865). The manifest features shared by the stories of Alice and Joan include total freedom from the laws of logic, time and space. But Méliès uses the Alice-like figure mainly in order to avoid the problem of Joan's sexuality. Her representation as a child enables Méliès to keep her in a "third zone" of asexuality, like the angels she meets in the field while daydreaming or in heaven. This device enables Méliès to locate Joan's story in the hagiographic tradition, without dealing with transvestitism as such.

We may conclude that all the retellings of the *Joan* story comprise a history of attempts to deny its problematic aspects and reduce it to a homogeneous system. Nevertheless, the inner core of the story – its heterogeneity and diverse femininity – are "smuggled" into various versions and disguises and thus pass into the history of culture from generation to generation.

In the many rewritings of the *Joan* myth, one of the "master knobs" (Hofstader, 1985 [1982]) that have been twisted and turned again and again over the centuries relates to the question of Joan's legitimacy. Luc Besson remarked, during an interview (Pivot, in *Antenne 2*, France), that what was most intriguing for him in the story was Joan's motivation: Why did she insist on continuing the fight when Charles, for his own political reasons, had decided to bring the battle to an end? Besson recognized here the central thread of the story and one of its cardinal moments. Charles's coronation ceremony symbolized the return not only of the monarch but of the patriarchal powers as well. From that moment on, Joan – who has received recognition for a limited period of time – gradually loses her powers. Her will to continue fighting, despite the fact that she has no army and can no longer hear her voices, results in her capture, her trial and, eventually, her death at the stake. Had Joan stopped fighting and returned to her village, her father and the sheep, she might have been saved. But then we would probably not have the *Joan* legend.

In all the retellings of the story, Joan's legitimacy was examined not only in terms of her social mobility but in terms of her gender as well. As both neutralized discourse (hagiographic and patriotic) and clinical-romantic discourse can testify, Joan's virginity (and androgyny) is not only the soft underbelly of the legend, but also its nuclear unit. Cinematic language by its nature turns the symbolic signs of verbal language into concrete signs. Thus, Joan's face, her forbidden body and her voices all acquire a physical presence of one kind or another. The important examination to confirm Joan's virginity was traditionally made behind the scenes, in both cinema and other cultural texts. She was examined by women who served the Church, and their decision as to whether she was a saint or a witch was final: only a virgin could serve as a messenger of God. Were she to be found "impure" – no further proof of her relations with the Devil was required.

Interestingly, in Jacques Rivette's version (1993), this scene is presented as part of the constructed world of the narrative.[5] Luc Besson goes even one step further when he locates the procedure at the very center of the scene. The examination becomes almost visible through the face of the courtyard mother-queen (Catherine Deneuve), the body language of the spectators and Joan's voices. This scene exposes the central mechanism of the Joan films as a mirror of patriarchal society.

The original Latin meaning of the word *speculum* was mirror, from *specere*, to look. But the speculum is also that concave mirror which gynecologists use to dilate and inspect the "cavity" of the female body (Luce Irigaray (1985 [1977] in Toril Moi, 1985: 130: "It is, paradoxically, through the imitation of its object that the speculum objectifies it in the first place" [ibid.]). As Irigaray has observed, the speculum is hollow, like the object it seeks to explore and it reflects the viewer's own point of view. Like Irigaray's *speculum*, the cinematic versions use selected discourses and repertoires of ready-made attributes as a focal point, as "a lens that can concentrate light rays so as to 'shed light on the secrets of caves and 'to pierce the mystery of the woman's sex'" (Irigaray, ibid.: 82, cited in Moi: 130). Since, like a concave mirror, the cinematic institution can represent Joan only according to its own reflection, it has devised a regime of discourse in order to manipulate and control Joan's problematic sexuality.

The apparatus that I have examined here seems to point toward "historical knowledge" as its desired object. Throughout hundreds of years, repetitive chains of displaced signals have marked the "source" as their imaginary object-cause and historical knowledge as a tool for rewriting and re-signifying the already known but repressed. As Michel de Certeau argues in *The Writing of History* (1988), "historical knowledge" is more about contemporary interests and identities and less about preserving the otherness of the past. In this sense, history functions as a tool by which one generation expresses its difference from its predecessors (ibid.: 46).The dialectic of sameness and difference in the Joan corpus posits, however, that all versions – classic and contemporary, manifest and disguised – are motivated by the same "otherness".

In the wake of Joan's problematic sexuality a rather rigid tradition emerged as to how to tell the story while remaining within the confines of propriety. Social and cultural structures dictated the repertoires available within these confines for selection in order to smuggle the story into history. At the same time, Western tradition has forced itself to add void narrative functions (the optional inventory) to hide the scandal of Joan's sexual diversity and the text's heterogeneity. This procedure represents the only possible way of telling the story while, at the same time, keeping its loose ends tied together. Hence, in a self-deluding fashion, the story of Joan of Arc in Western culture pretends to be about the legitimization of feminine social dynamism (secular and religious). In fact, however, it is a story about Western culture's self-censorship; it is a nightmare that culture seeks to purge by retelling it again and again, without waking up. For a conditional time, and in a limited space, Joan was allowed to cross the border between men and women. But when, at the coronation, the clock struck twelve, figuratively speaking, she was expected to return to her sheep in the village. Years after her martyrdom at the stake, she was declared a saint and a patriot, but her activism and her transvestitism have never been forgiven.

III   Fetishism and Exorcism

On the face of it, Joan of Arc is Carmen's diametrical opposite: a pure, young virgin, motivated by the highest of callings – God and Country – whereas Carmen is draped in the glamour of the gypsy band and the bullring to the accompaniment (usually) of what is certainly some of the most tantalizing music ever written. However, both Carmen and Joan are acting in the twilight zones between masculinity and femininity, and legitimacy and non-legitimacy. Each in her own way is a female figure who defies social conventions and is executed as a result. In each chain of cinematic repetitions, their voices are muted, their legitimacy is questioned and their forbidden sexual independence is an object for borrowed images, stereotypes and a variety of discourses.

Culture's recurrent preoccupation with the same texts delineates a problematic area within the master narrative. In *Gynesis: Configuration of Woman and Modernity*, Alice Jardine claims that the "feminine" signifies not woman herself, but those "spaces which could be said to conceptualize the master narrative's 'non-knowledge,' that area over which the narrative has lost control" (1985: 24). This is the primordial unknown, the terrifying, the disturbing hole which culture has to clarify.

Julia Kristeva (1982) uses the term "abjected" for that which does not "respect borders, positions, rules," that which "disturbs identity, system, order" (ibid.: 4, in Creed, 1986: 45). According to Kristeva, various rituals become means by which patriarchal societies first renew their initial contact with abject elements and then exclude them (see Creed, ibid.). Obstinate cinematic remakes might be included among these kinds of rituals. Both the search for a bypass to the male Symbolic order (the phallus) and the violation of the central role of woman as procreative agent must be repeated in order to achieve their narrative denouement – the death of the female rebel. Through a process of appropriation, phallocentric society signals its borderlines (see also Lucy Fischer, 1979-80, Alice Jardine, 1985 and Barbara Creed, 1986). The transformations of *Joan of Arc* and *Carmen* in the course of cinema history represent the forbidden spaces where the womb ceases to function as a generative vessel and where woman refuses to conform to the symbolic order. While using the dialectic of repetitions and differences as their motivating force, these persistently performative rewritings are marked "holes" in the symbolic order. This unresolved enigma in the master narrative, repeated in diverse transformations of femininity as "elsewhereness," probably percolates through other cinematic products. It would be interesting for future research to trace more hidden or "black" versions of *Carmen* and *Joan of Arc*, like BREAKING THE WAVES or ALIEN III, which camouflage the same enigmatic anxiety and continue the same ritual of abjection.

By way of repetition, we may conclude that the cinema as a social institution knows what Scheherazade seems to have known all along: to narrate is to triumph over death. Thus, in an ongoing ceremony that occurs in the darkness of the movie theater (and ultimately lasts more than 1001 nights), Marion and Susanna, Carmen, Joan, Beth and Ripley are encoded messages that society constantly delivers to its members. By ritualistically exorcizing them again and again, society delineates areas of denial. At the same time, every new version testifies to the urgency of their relevance. Since every reading is a rewriting, however, and since, following Žižek, "the gaze is [...] a point at which the very frame [of my view] is already inscribed in the 'content' of the picture view" (1991: 125), this reading might by itself serve, as it were, as yet another version.

Notes

1. To repeat here Rosalind Krauss's title: "Originality as Repetition [...]" (1986).
2. The *dominant* was defined by the Russian Formalists as the focusing component of the work of art through which the hierarchical structure of devices is achieved (Roman Jakobson 1971 [1935] in McHale, 1987: 6-7).
3. In McHale 1987: 7.
4. Where it connotes the adventure and mystery associated with a young, brave and beautiful woman.
5. See also Yervasi (1999).

References

Abel, Richard (1984) *French Cinema: The First Wave, 1915-1929*. New Jersey: Princeton University Press

Acocella, Joan (1999) "Joan of Arc" in: *The New Yorker* (A Critic at Large), November 15, 1999: 98-105

Agee, James and Evans, Walker (1941) *Let Us Now Praise Famous Men*. Boston. Mass.: Houghton-Mifflin

Agel, Henri (1985) 'La Jeanne d'Arc de Dreyer' in: *Les Cahiers de la Cinémathèque: Revue d'Histoire du Cinéma*: (Le Moyen Age au cinéma) vol. 42/43: 45-49

Amossy, Ruth (2002) "Introduction to the Study of Doxa" in: *Poetics Today* 23(3): 369-394

Ankersmit, Frank R. (1994) *History and Tropology: The Rise and Fall of Metaphor*. Berkeley, Los Angeles and London: University of California Press

Aquin, Stephane (2001) "Hitchcock et l'art contemporain" pp. 173-178 in: "Paini Dominique & Cogeval Guy, 2001, *Hitchcock et l'art: coïncidences fatales*. Paris: Centre Pompidou, Mazzotta

Astre, G.A. and Estève, M. (eds.) (1962) *Jeanne d'Arc à l'écran, Études Cinématographiques*. vol. 18-19, Paris: M.J. Minard

Bal, Mieke (1993) "His Master's Eye" in: *Modernity and the Hegemony of Vision*. Berkley, Los Angeles and London: University of California Press pp. 379-404

Balázs, Béla (1952) "The Face of Men" in *Theory of the Film: Character and Growth of a New Art*. Translated by Edith Bone. London

Barret, W.P. (ed.) (1931) *The Trial of Jeanne d'Arc*. A Complete Translation with an Introduction. London: George Routledge

Barthes, Roland (1974 [1970]) *S/Z*. Translated by Richard Miller. Preface by Richard Howard. New York: Hill and Wang

— (1975 [1973]) *The Pleasure of the Text*. Translated by Richard Miller. Preface by Richard Howard. New York: Farrar, Straus and Giroux, Inc.

— (1977) [1964]) "Rhetoric of the Image" in: *Image-Music-Text*. Essays selected and trans. Stephen Heath, London: Fontana/Collins pp. 33-52

— (1977 [1966]) "Introduction to the Structural Analysis of Narratives" in: *Image-Music-Text*. Essays selected and translated by Stephene Heath, pp. 79-125. London: Fontana/ Collins

— (1977 [1961]) "The Photographic Message" in: *Image-Music-Text*. Essays selected and translated by Stephen Heath, London: Fontana/Collins pp. 15-32

— (1977) *Fragments d'un discours amoureux*. Paris: Éditions du Seuil

— (1986 [1967]) "The Discourse of History" in: *The Rustle of Language,* translated by Richard Howard pp. 149-57. London: Basil Blackwell

Batchelor, Jennifer (1984) "From 'Aida' to 'Zauberflöte' (The Opera Film)" in: *Screen*: 25(3) May-June 1984 pp. 26-38

Baudrillard, Jean (1980) *Simulations*. Translated by Paul Foss and Poul Patton, New York: Semiotext[e]

— (1983) *In the Shadow of the Silent Majorities, or The End of the Social and Other Essays*. Translated by Paul Foss. John Johnston and Paul Patton. New York: Semiotext[e] Foreign Agents Series

Baudry, Jean-Louis (1985 [1970]) "Ideological Effects of the Basic Cinematographic Apparatus" reprinted in: *Movies & Methods*. Ed. by Bill Nichols. Vol. II. pp. 531-543. Los Angeles, Berkley and London: California UP, 1985

Bazin, André (1967 [1950, 1955]) "The Evolution of the Language of Cinema" in: *What is Cinema*. Trans. Hugh Gray. Berkeley: University of California Press pp. 23-40

Bellour, Raymond (1974 [1971]) "The Unattainable Text" in: *Screen* 16(3): 19-27. (1979) "Cine-Repetitions" in: *Screen* 20(2) 65-72

— (1979) "Psychosis, Neurosis, Perversion" in: *Camera Obscura* Summer 1979: pp. 104-132

Benjamin, Walter (1969 [1936]) "The Work of Art in the Age of Mechanical Reproduction" in: *Illuminations* Edited by Hannah Arendt. Translated by Harry Zohn. New York: Schocken Books

Ben-Porat, Ziva (1983) "Modern Literary Imitations and Semiotics of Culture" in: *Proceedings of the Second Congress of Semiotic Studies* Vienna 1979, Den Haag: Mouton pp. 733-740

— (1985) "Intertextuality, Rhetorical Intertexuality, Allusion and Parody" [Hebrew] in: *Ha-sifrout* 34(2): 170-79, Tel-Aviv

Berger, John (1977) *Ways of Seeing*. New York: Penguin

Bernheimer, Charles (1989) "Manet's *Olympia*: The Figuration of the Scandal", in: *Poetics Today* 10(2): 255-77

Berthier, Philip (2001) "Les vocations d'Orphée" in: Bricout, Bernadette (ed.) *Le regard d'Orphée* pp. 35-56. Paris: Edition du Seuil

Bhabha, Homi, K (1990 [1986]) "The Other Question: Difference, Discrimination and the Discourse of Colonialism" in: *Out There: Marginalization and Contemporary Cultures*. Ed. by Russell Ferguson et al. pp. 71-87. Cambridge, Massachusetts & London, England: MOMA & MIT Press.

— (1998) "The White Stuff (Political Aspect of Whiteness)" in: *Artforum* 36(9) May 1998: 21-24

Bhabha, Homi & Burgin Victor (1994) "Visualizing theory: 'in dialogue'" in: *Visualizing Theory: Selected Essays from VAR 1990-1994*. Ed. by Lucien Taylor, New York: Routledge

Biancoli, Louis (ed.) (1953) *The Opera Reader: A Complete Guide to the Best-Loved Operas* pp. 70-79.New York: Grosset and Dunlop

Biancoli, Louis & Bayer Robert (1953) *The Victor Book of Operas*. Revised edition pp. 60-72. New York: Simon & Schuster

Bizet, Georges (1875) *Carmen, Opera in Four Acts*. Libretto by Henri Meilhac and Ludvic Halevy. Orchestre National de France. Choeurs et maitraise de radio France. Conducted by Seiji Ozawa Philips Classic Production (1988)

Blaetz, Robin (1989) "Jeanne d'Arc au cinéma" in: *Association des amis du centre Jeanne d'Arc*, Orléans. Bulletin (13): 29-39

Bloom, Harold (1977 [1973]) *The Anxiety of Influence: A Theory of Poetry*. Oxford and New York: Oxford University Press

Bordwell, David (1981) *The Films of Carl-Theodor Dreyer*. Especially "La Passion de Jeanne d'Arc" pp. 66-93. Berkeley and Los Angeles: University of California Press

— (1989) "Rhetoric in Action: Seven Models of PSYCHO" in: *Making Meaning: Inference and Rhetoric in the Interpretation of Cinema*. Cambridge, Mass & London, England: Harvard University Press pp. 224-248

Bourdieu, Pierre (1971) "Le marche des biens symboliques" in: *L'Anneé sociologique* vol. (22): 49-126

— (1990) *In Other Words: Essays Towards a Reflexive Sociology*. Trans. Matthew Adamson. Stanford: Stanford University Press

Bourdieu, Pierre & Passeron, Jean-Claude (1977) *Reproduction in Education Society and Culture* Trans. Richard Nice. Beverly Hills, California: Sage

Bouzy, Olivier (1999) "Le cinéaste et son public, Jeanne d'Arc et L'historian" in: *Association des amis du centre Jeanne d'Arc*. Orléans. Bulletin (23): 3-27

Bremond, Claude (1985) "Concept et theme" in: *Poétique: du theme en littérature* Vol. 64. Paris: Édition du Seuil

Bronfen, Elisabeth (1996 [1992]) *Over Her Dead Body*. Manchester: Manchester University Press

Butler, Judith (1993) *Bodies That Matter*. London and New York: Routledge

Carroll, Noël (1990) *The Philosophy of Horror or Paradoxes of the Heart*. New York and London: Routledge

— (1996) *Theorizing the Moving Image*. New York Cambridge University Press

— (1998 [1982]) "The Future of Allusion: Hollywood in the Seventies and Beyond" in: *Interpreting the Moving Image*. New York: Cambridge University Press pp. 240-264

Cartmeli, Deborah & Whelehan Imelda (eds.) (1999) *Adaptations: From Text to Screen, Screen to Text.* London and New York: Routledge

Champion, Pierre (1920) *Notice des manuscrits du Procès de rehabilitation de Jeanne d'Arc.* Paris: Librairie Honoré Champion

Cheshine, Godfrey (1998) "'PSYCHO's Analysis: Van Sant's Remake Slavish But Sluggish" in: *Variety* Mon., Dec. 7, 1998

Chion, Michel (1998) "The *Acousmêtre*" in: *The Voice in Cinema* New York: Columbia University Press

Clark, Timothy J. (1980) "Preliminaries to a Possible Treatment of *Olympia*" in: *Screen* 21(1): 18-41

Clément, Catherine (1989 [1986]) *Opera or the Undoing of Women.* Translated by Betsy Wing. Foreword by Susan McClary. London: Virago Press

Creed, Barbara (1986)"Horror and the Monstrous Feminine: An Imaginary Abjection" in: *Screen* 1: 44-70

Cole, Abimbola, 2002, "From Georges Bizet to Robert Townsend: Deconstructing Images of Carmen". Paper presented at the Carmen Conference Centre for Research into Film & Media. University of Newcastle upon Tyne

Dällenbach, Lucien (1976) "Intertexte et autotexte" in: *Poétique*, vol. 27: 282-297

— (1989) *The Mirror in the Text.* Trans. by Jeremy Whiteley with Emma Hughes. Chicago: Chicago University Press

De Certeau, Michel (1984) *The Practice of Everyday Life.* Trans. by Steven Randall. Berkeley: University of California Press

Deleuze, Gilles (1994 [1968]) *Difference and Repetition.* Translated by Paul Patton. New York: Columbia University Press

Deleuze, Gilles R. and Felix Guattari (1986) *Kafka.* Minneapolis: University of Minnesota Press

— 1987 (1980) *A Thousand Plateaus: Capitalism and Schizophrenia.* Translated and foreword by Brian Massumi. Minneapolis & London: University of Minnesota Press

Deren, Maya (1953) "Poetry and the Film". A Symposium organized by *Cinema 16.* October 1953

Dika, Vera (2003) *Recycled Culture in Contemporary Art and Film: The Uses of Nostalgia.* Cambridge, UK & New York, USA: Cambridge University Press

Doane, Mary Ann (1982) "Film and the Masquerade: Theorizing the Female Spectator" in: *Screen* 23(3-4): 74-87

— (1985) "Medical Discourses in the 'Women's Film' of the 1940s" in: *Poetics Today* 6(1-2): 205-227

— [(1986) 1980] "The Voice in the Cinema: The Articulation of Body and Space," in: *Narrative, Apparatus, Ideology: A Film Theory Reader,* edited by Philip Rosen, 335-49. New York: Columbia University Press

Donaldson, Peter, S (1996) "The Shakespeare Interactive Archive: New Directions in Electronic Scholarship on Text and Performance" in: *Contexualizing Media* ed. By Ed Barret. Cambridge: MIT pp. 103-127

Donington, Robert (1978) *The Opera*. Especially chapter 11: "France, Russia and Italy" pp. 169-178. New York: Harcourt, Brace, Jovanovich

Eberwein, Robert (1998) "Remakes and Cultural Studies" in: *Play It Again, Sam*: *Retakes on Remakes*. Edited by Andrew Horton & Stuart Y. McDougal. With an afterword by Leo Braudy. Berkeley, Los Angeles & London: University of California Press: 15-33

Eco, Umberto (1983) *The Name of the Rose*. Translated by William Weaver San Diego, New York and London: Harcourt, Brace, Jovanovich

— (1985) "Innovation and Repetition: Between Modern and Post-Modern Aesthetics" in: *Daedalus* 114(4): 161-84

— (1988 [1984]) "Casablanca, Cult Movies and Intertextual Collage" in: *Travels in Hypereality*, London: Picador pp. 197-211

Elsaesser, Thomas (2001) "The Blockbuster: Everything Connects but Not Everything Goes" in: Jon Lewis (ed.) *The End of Cinema as We Know It: American Film in the Nineties*. New York, London: New York University, pp. 11-22

Encyclopedia Britannica (1954) A New Survey of Universal Knowledge. Vol. 13: pp. 72-75. Chicago, London, Toronto Encyclopedia Britannica INC. founded 1768

Estève, Michel (ed.) (1962) *Études cinématographiques: Jeanne d'Arc a l'écran*. Paris. Volume 18-19

Even-Zohar, Itamar (1990 [1979]) "Polysystem Theory" in: *Poetics Today* 11(1): 9-27

— (1990 [1982]) "Reality and Realemes in Narrative" in: *Poetics Today* 11(1): 207-18

Everyman's Encyclopedia (1967 [1958]) vol. 7.: 214. London: J.M. Dent & Sons Ltd. Fifth edition

Feldman, Avigdor (1991) "The Sirens' Songs: Discourse and Space in the Court of Justice" in: *Theory and Criticism*. An Israel Forum, Summer, 1991(1): 143-163. Van Leer Institute, Jerusalem [Hebrew]

Fischer, Lucy (1979) "The Lady Vanished: Women, Magic and the Movies" in: *Film Quarterly* 33(1): 22-34

— (1989) *Shot/Counter Shot: Film Tradition and Women's Cinema*. Princeton, NJ: Princeton University Press

Foucault, Michel (1972 [1969]) *The Archaeology of Knowledge*. Translated by Alan Sheridan, New York: Random House

— (1976) *Histoire de la Sexualité*. Vol. I Paris: Gallimard

— (1977 [1969]) *Language, Counter-Memory, Practice: Selected Essays and Interviews*. Edited by Donald F. Bouchard. Translated by Sherry Simon. Oxford: Basil Blackwell

— (1986) "Of Other Space" in: *Diacritics* 16(1) pp. 22-29

— (2004 [1971]) *La peinture de Manet (Suivi de Michel Foucault, un regard)*. Sous La direction de Maryvonne Saiaon. Paris: Editions du Seuil pp. 21-47

Fowles, John (1985) *A Maggot*. London and Sydney: Pan Books

Freedman, A. & Kaplan, H. (1967) (eds.) "Schizophrenic Reactions" in: *Comprehensive Textbook of Psychiatry* pp. 593-649. Baltimore: The William and Wilkins Company

Freud, Sigmund (1907) "Delusions and Dreams in Jensen's *Gradiva*" in: *The Standard Edition of the Complete Psychological Works of Sigmund Freud*, vol. 9. London: Hogarth Press, 1953-1974

— (1955 [1920]) "Beyond the Pleasure Principle" in: *The Standard Edition of the Complete Psychological Work of Sigmund Freud* vol. 18, 24-33. London: Hogarth Press

Friedman, Régine Michal (1996) "La spécularité diffractée: Mise-en-abyme et début de film" in: *Semiotica* 112 (1-2): 51-65

— (1998) "Generations of the Aftermath: The Parodic Mode" Blurred Boundaries-Assaph Studies in Cinema & Television Tel-Aviv University, Faculty of the Arts.1: 71-82

Furman, Nelly (1988) "The Language of Love in Carmen" in: *Reading Opera* A. Gross and R. Parker (eds.) New Jersey: Princeton University Press pp. 168-183

— (2002) "Carmen in Black and White". Paper presented at the Carmen Conference Center for Research into Film & Media. University of Newcastle upon Tyne, England

Gabriel, Teshome, H (1990) "Thoughts on Nomadic Aesthetics and Black Independent Cinema: Traces of a Journey" in: *Out There Marginalization and Contemporary Cultures*. Ed. by Russell Ferguson et al. pp. 395-410. Cambridge, Massachusetts & London, England: MOMA & The MIT Press

Garrard, Mary D. (1982) "Artemisia and Susanna" pp. 147-171 in: Broude Norma & Garrard Mary (eds.) *Feminism and Art History: Questioning the Litany*. New York: Harper & Row Publishers

Genette, Gérard (1982) *Palimpsestes: La littérature au second degré*. Paris: Éditions du Seuil

Gies, Frances (1981) *Joan of Arc: The Legend and the Reality*. New York: Harper & Row

Gilad, Moshe (1985) *Ontology and Historical Fiction.* Thesis submitted for the degree of MA. Supervised by Brian McHale. Department of Poetics and Comparative Literature, Tel Aviv University

Golea, Antoine (1975) "Commentary", to Bizet's *Carmen*, directed by Alain Lambard. Philharmonic Orchestra of Strasbourg. France: Costallat

Grand Dictionaire Encyclopédique Larousse (1984) vol. 6: 343-345. Paris: Librarie Larousse

Greimas, A.J. (1977 [1969]) "Elements of a Narrative Grammar" in: *Diacritics* (7): 40-73

Harmand, Adrien (1929) *Jeanne d'Arc: ses costumes, son armure. Essai de reconstitution.* Paris: Librarie Ernest Leroux

Harris, Kenneth Marc (1992) *The Film Fetish.* New York, San Francisco, Bern, Baltimore, Berlin, Paris: Peter Lang

Hernstein Smith, Barbara (1980) "Afterthought on Narrative-Narrative Versions, Narrative Theories" in: *Critical Inquiry* Autumn, 1980, 213-236

Higashi, Sumiko (1994) *Cecil B. DeMille and American Culture: The Silent Era.* Berkeley, Los Angeles and London: University of California Press

Hofstadter, D.R. (1985a [1982]) "Variations on a Theme as the Crux of Creativity", in: *Metamagical Themes: Questing for Essence of Mind and Pattern* pp. 232-259. New York: Penguin

— (1985b [1982]) "Metafont, Metamathematics and Metaphysics: Comment on Donald Knuth's Article 'The Concept of Meta-Font'" in *Metamagical Themes: Questing for Essence of Mind and Pattern* pp. 260-296. New York: Penguin

Horton Andrew & McDougal, Stuart Y. (eds.) (1998) *Play it Again, Sam.* University of California Press, Berkeley & Los Angeles, California

Hrushovsky, Benjamin (1982) "An Outline of Integrational Semantics" in: *Poetics Today* 3(4): 59-88

Hutcheon, Linda (1989) *The Politics of Postmodernism.* London & New York: Routledge

Huyssen, Andreas (1986) *After the Great Divide: Modernism, Mass Culture, Postmodernism.* Bloomington and Indianapolis: Indiana University Press

Iordanova, Dina.(2000) *"Before the Rain* in a Balkan context" in: *Rethinking History* vol. 4(2) pp. 147-156

— (2001) *Cinema of Flames: Balkan film, Culture and Media.* London: British Film Institute

Irigarey, Luce (1985 [1977]) "This Sex which is Not One" in: *This Sex which is Not One.* New York: Cornell University Press

Jakobson, Roman (1960) "Linguistics and Poetry" in: *Style and Language* Edited by T.A. Sebeok Cambridge, Mass: MIT Press pp. 350-377
— (1971 [1935]) "The Dominant", in: *Readings in Russian Poetics: Formalist and Structuralist Views*. Edited by Matejka Ladislav and Kristine Pomorska. Cambridge, MA and London: MIT Press
Jameson, Frederic (1981) *The Political Unconscious*. Ithaca: Cornell University Press
Jardine, Alice (1985) *Gynesis: Configuration of Woman and Modernity*. Ithaca and London: Cornell University Press

Kaes, Anton (1990) "History and Film: Public Memory in the Age of Electronic Dissemination" in: *History and Memory* 2(1) Fall: 111-129
Klinger, Barbara (1982) "*Psycho*: The Institutionalization of Female Sexuality" in: *Wide Angle* (5): 49-55
Kochberg, Searle (1996) "Cinema as Institution" in: *An Introduction to Film Studies*, Second Edition. Ed. by Jill Nelmes, London and New York: Routledge
Krauss, Rosalind (1986) "Originality as Repetition: Introduction" in: *October* Summer 1986 (37): 35-40. MIT
— (2000) "*A Voyage on the North Sea*": *Art in the Age of the Post-Medium Condition*. London: Thames & Hudson
Kristeva, Julia (1982) *Powers of Horror: An Essay on Abjection*. New York: Columbia University Press

Labov, William (1975 [1972]) "The Transformation of Experience in Narrative Syntax" in: *Language in the Inner City: Studies in the Black English Vernacular*. Philadelphia: University of Pennsylvania Press
Lacan, Jacques (1977) "The Seminar, Book XI" in: *The Four Fundamental Concept of Psychoanalysis*. Translated by Alan Sheridan. London: Hogarth Press and the Institute of Psychoanalysis
— (1982 [1966]) *Ecrits: A Selection*. Translated by Alan Sheridan London: Tavistock Publications
Lacombe, Herve (1999) "The Writing of Exoticism in the Libretti of the *Opera-Comique, 1825-1862*" in: *Cambridge Opera Journal*, 11(2): 135-158
Lany, Michel (1987) *Jeanne d'Arc-histoire vraie et genèse d'un mythe*. Paris: Payot
Lefebvre, Henri (1991[1974]) *The Production of Space*. Translated by Donald Nicholson-Smith. Oxfords, UK & Cambridge, USA: Blackwell
Lefebvre, Martin (1997) *Psycho: De la figure au musée imaginaire-théorie et pratique de l'acte de spectature*. Paris: L'Harmattan, Collection Champs Visuels
Leitch, Thomas M. (1990) "The Rhetoric of the Remake" in: *Literature/Film Quarterly* Vol. 18/3 November 1990 pp. 138-149

— (2000) "101 Ways to Tell Hitchcock's *Psycho* from Gus Van Sant's" in: *Literature & Film Quarterly* Vol. 28: 4 pp. 269-273

Leprohon, Pierre (1962) "Les premières images se Jeanne d'Arc à l'écran" in: *Études cinématographiques: Jeanne d'Arc à l'écran* vol. 18-19: 38-39

Levinas, Emmanuel (1969 [1961]) *Totality and Infinity: An Essay on Exteriority.* Translated by Alphonso Lingis. Pittsburgh: Duquesne University Press

Lévi-Strauss, Claude (1979 [1958]) "The Structural Study of Myth" in: *Structural Anthropology.* Trans. by C. Jacobson & B.G. Schoepf, vol. I: chapter 11 pp. 206- Harmondsworth: Penguin

Limbacher, L. James (1991) *Haven't I Seen You Somewhere Before? Remakes, Sequels, and Series in Motion Pictures, Videos and Television, 1986-1990.* Ann Arbor: The Pierian Press

Linderman, Deborah (1986) "Uncoded Images in the Heterogeneous Text" in: Philip Rosen (ed.) *Narrative, Apparatus, Ideology.* New York: Columbia University Press. pp. 143-152

Lockspeiser, Edward (1967-8) "Bizet and *Carmen*", comments on *Carmen*-Opera in Four Acts by Georges Bizet. Book by Henri Meilhac & Ludovic Halévy. Based on the Story by Prosper Mérimée. Conducted by Herbert von Karajan

Lotman, J.M. (1975) "On the Meta language of a Typological Description of Culture" in: *Semiotica* (14)2: 97-123

Lotman, J. and B.A. Uspensky (1978) "On the Semiotic Mechanism of Culture," in: *New Literary History*

Lyotard, Jean-François (1978 [1976]) "On the Strength of the Weak" in: *Semiotext [e]* 3(2): 204-14

Maingueneau, Dominique (1984) *Carmen: Les racines d'un mythe.* Paris: Edition du Sorbier

Malraux, André (1951) *Les Voix du silence.* Paris: Gallimard

Malthête, Jacques (1996) *Méliès: Images et illusions.* Paris: Exporégie

Marchand, Jean (1955) *Le Procès de Condamnation de Jeanne d'Arc. Reproduction en fac-similé du manuscrit authentique sur vélin no. 1191 de la Bibliothèque de l'Assemblée Nationale.* Introduction by Jean Marchant. Paris: Plon

Margolis, Nadia (1990) *Joan of Arc in History, Literature and Film: An Annotated Bibliography.* New York & London: Garland

Maxwell, F. Ronald (2000) *"The Messenger"* in: *History Today.* April 2000(50)4: 52- 53

McClary, Susan (1997) "Structures of Identity and Difference in Bizet's *Carmen*" in: Richard Dellamora & Daniel Fischlin (eds.) *The Work of Opera: Genre, Nationhood, and Sexual Difference* pp. 115-129. New York: Columbia University Press

— (2002) "Carmen as Perennial Fusion: From *Habañera* to Hip-Hop". Paper presented at the Carmen Conference Center for Research into Film & Media. University of Newcastle upon Tyne

McDougal, Stuart Y. (1998) "The Director Who Knew Too Much: Hitchcock Remakes Himself" in: Horton, Andrew & Stuart Y. McDougal (eds.) *Play It Again Sam: Retakes on Remakes*. Los Angeles, Berkeley and London: University of California Press

McFarlane, Brian (1996) *Novel to Film: An Introduction to the Theory of Adaptation*. Oxford: Clarendon Press

McHale, Brian (1985) "L'abîme américan: pour une théorie systématique de la fiction américain" in: *Littérature* 57: 48-65

— (1986) "Change of Dominant from Modernist to Postmodernist Writing" in: *Approaching Postmodernism: Papers Presented at a Workshop on Postmodernism* (ed.) Douwe Fokkema, 53-79. Utrecht: University of Utrecht

— (1987) *Postmodernist Fiction*. New York: Methuen

Megill, Alan (1985) *Prophets of Extremity: Nietzsche, Heidegger, Foucault, Derrida*. London, Berkeley and Los Angeles: University of California Press

Melberg, Arne (1990) "Repetition (In the Kierkegaardian Sense of the Term)" in: *Diacritics*, Fall 1990 vol. 20(3): 71-87

Meltzer, Françoise (2001) *For Fear of the Fire: Joan of Arc and the Limits of Subjectivity*. Distributed for the University of Chicago Press

Mérimée, Prosper. 1963 (1845) *"Carmen"* in: *Carmen, Colombia and Selected Stories*. Translated by Walter J. Cobb, 17-73. Foreword by George Steiner. A Signet Classic. USA: New American Library

— 1990 (1845) *Carmen and Other Stories*. Translated and edited with a forward by Nicholas Jotcham. Oxford University Press

Metz, Christian (1974) *Language and Cinema*. Translated by Donna Jean Umiker Sebeok. The Hague: Mouton

— (1975) "The Imaginary Signifier". Translated by Ben Brewster in: *Screen* 16 (2): 46-76

— (1976 [1971]) "On the Notion of Cinematographic Language". Translated by Diane Abramo in: *Movies & Methods*, edited by Bill Nichols, vol. 1: 582-89. Berkeley and Los Angeles: University of California Press

Michaud-Fréjaville, Françoise (2001) "Cinéma, Histoire: Autour du theme 'Johannique'" in: *Le Moyen Age: vu par le cinema European. Les cahiers de conques*, no.3. Centre Européen d'Art et de Civilisation Médiévale pp. 161-183

Moi, Toril (1991 [1985]) *Sexual/ Textual Politics: Feminist Literary Theory*. London and New York: Routledge

Mulvey, Laura (1975) "Visual Pleasure and Narrative Cinema" in: *Screen* 16(3): 6-18

Murphy, Kathleen (1992) "The Last Temptation of Sigourney Weaver" in: *Film Comment* vol. 28: 17-20

Nabokov, Vladimir (1981 [1955]) *Lolita.* New York: Penguin Books

Naficy, Hamid (1993) "Exile Discourse and Televisual Fetishization" in: Hamid Naficy and Teshome H. Gabriel (eds.), *Otherness and the Media: The Ethnography of the Imagined and the Imaged* pp. 85-116. USA, Switzerland and Australia: Harwood Academic Publishers

Naremore, James (ed.) (2000) *Film Adaptation.* New Jersey: Rutgers University Press

Neale, (Steve) Stephen (1980) *Genre.* London: BFI

— (1985) *Cinema and Technology: Image, Sound, Color* BFI & Macmillan Ltd: London and Basingstoke

— (1990) "Questions of Genre" in: *Screen* (31)1: 45-66

Owens, Craig (1984) "The Discourse of Others: Feminism and Postmodernism" in: *The Anti-Aesthetics: Essays on Postmodern Culture* (ed.) Hal Foster. Port Townsend, Washington: Bay Press

Païni, Dominique & Cogeval, Guy (eds.) (2000) *Hitchcock et l'Art: Coïncidences Fatales.* Quebec, Milano & Paris: Centre Pompidou and Mazzota

Pavel, Thomas (1981) "Tragedy and the Sacred: Notes Towards a Semantic Characterization of a Fictional Genre" in: *Poetics* 10: 2-3

Pernoud, Régine (1955) (ed.) *The Retrial of Joan of Arc: The Evidence at the Trial for Her Rehabilitation.* Trans. J.M. Cohen, New York: Harcourt, Brace and Company

— (1985) "Jeanne d'Arc à l'écran" in: *Les cahiers de la cinémathèque Revue d'Histoire du cinéma* (Le Moyen Age au cinéma) 42/43: 40-42

— (1994) *J'ai nom Jeanne la Pucelle.* Decouverts Gallimard-Histoire

Pernoud, Régine and Clin Marie-Véronique (1998 [1986]) *Joan of Arc: Her Story.* Trans. Jeremy du Quesnay Adams. New York: St. Martin's Griffin

Pipolo, Tony (1988) "The Spectre of Joan of Arc: Textual Variations in the Key Prints of Carl Dreyer's Films" in: *Film History* (2): 301-24

Pithon, Rémy (1985) "Joan of Arc de Victor Fleming: de la résistance à la nuée" in: *Les cahiers de la cinémathèque: Reuve d'Histoire du cinéma (Le Moyen Age au cinéma)* (ed.) François de la Bretèque. (42/43): 50-58

Powrie, Phil (2004) "Politics and Embodiment in: *Karmen Geï*" *Quarterly Review of Film and Video* (21): 283-291

Praz, Mario (1970 [1951]) *The Romantic Agony.* Translated by Angus Davidson. London and New York

Prescott, J.R.V. (1987) *Political Frontiers and Boundaries.* Boston, Sydney & Wellington: Unwin Hyman

Protopopoff, Daniel (1989a) "Qu'est-ce qu'un remake" in: *CinémAction: Le remake et L'adaptation* 53: 13-17

— (1989b) "'Dracula, Robin des bois, Tarzan ... Les variantes du mythe cinématographique" in: *CinémAction: Le remake et L'adaptation* (53): 48-54

— (1989c) "Les *Carmen* de l'écran" in: *CinémAction: Le remake et L'adaptation* (53): 55-63

Protopopoff, Daniel & Michel Serceau (1989) "Faux remakes et vraies adaptations" in: *CinémAction: Le remake et L'adaptation* (53): 37-45

Raknem, Ingvald (1971) *Joan of Arc in History, Legend and Literature.* Scandinavian University Books: Universitetsfolaget

Rebello, Stephen (1998 [1990]) *Alfred Hitchcock and the Making of Psycho.* New York: St. Martin's

Reff, Theodore (1977) *Manet: Olympia.* New York: Viking

Riffaterre, Michel (1980) "Syllepsis" in: *Critical Inquiry* 6(4): 625-38

Rogoff, Irit (2000) *Terra Infirma: Geography's Visual Culture.* London & New York: Routledge

Rosenstone, Robert A. (1995) *Vision of the Past: the Challenge of Film to Our Idea of History.* Cambridge, Mass: Harvard University Press

— (1996) "The Future of the Past: Film and the beginning of Postmodern history" in: Vivian Sobchack (ed.) *The Persistence of History* pp. 201-218. AFI Film Readers, New York and London: Routledge

— (2000) "A History of What Has Not Yet Happened" in: *Rethinking History* 4 (1): 183-192

Rothman, William (1982) *Hitchcock-The Murderous Gaze.* Harvard University Press: Cambridge, Massachusetts, & London, England

— (1999) "Some Thoughts on Hitchcock's Authorship" in: *Alfred Hitchcock – Centenary Essays.* Edited by Richard Allen & S. Ishii-Gonzalès pp. 29-42. London: BFI Publishing. 1999

Rusen, Jörn (1987) "Historical Narration: Foundation, Types, Reason" in: *History and Theory: Studies in the Philosophy of History.* Wesleyan University Press

Said, Edward W. (1979) *Orientalism.* New York: Random House

Sarris, Andrew (1996 [1968]) *The American Cinema: Directors and Directions 1929-1968.* USA: Da Capo Press

Scahill, John H. (1993) "Meaning-Construction and Habitus". Proceedings of the Forty-Ninth Annual Meeting of the Philosophy of Education Society. University of Illinois. http: //www.ed.uiuc.edu/EPS/PES-Yearbook/93_docs/SCAHILL.HTM

Schutz, William Todd (1999) "Off-Stage Voices in James Agee's *Let Us Now Praise Famous Men*: Reportage as Covert Autobiography" in: *American Imago* 56(1): 75-104

Shakespeare, William (1981 [1623]) *King Henry VI, Part I*. Edited by Andrew S. Cairncross. The Arden Edition of the Works of William Shakespeare. London, New York: Methuen

Shapiro, Owen & Pedro Cuperman (1990) "The Fascination of Ulysses: Music in Film. A Study of Music's Central Role in the Semiological Relation between Artistic Message and Reception". Unpublished manuscript, Syracuse University

Shaw, Bernard (1980 [1921]) *Saint Joan. A Chronicle Play in Six Scenes and Epilogue*. London: Penguin Books

Shohat, Ella (1993) "Gender and Culture of Empire: Toward a Feminist Ethnography of the cinema" in: *Otherness and the Media- the Ethnography of the Imagined and the Imaged*. Ed. by Hamid Naficy & Teshome H. Gabriel pp. 45-84. USA, Switzerland, Australia: Harwood Academic Publishers

Smith, Jeff (2003) "Black Faces, White Voices: The Politics of Dubbing in *Carmen Jones*" in: *The Velvet Light Trap* (51): 29-42

Sobchack, Vivian (1995 [1990]) "'Surge and Splendor': A Phenomenology of the Hollywood Historical Epic" in: Barry Keith Grant (ed.) *Film Genre Reader II* pp. 280-307. Austin: University of Texas Press

Sorlin, Pierre (1980) *The Film in History: Restaging the Past*. Oxford: Blackwell

Spivak, Gayatri Chakravotry (1985) "Can the Subaltern Speak? Speculations on Widow Sacrifice" in: *Wedge* 7/8 120-30

Spoto, Donald (2001) "Hitchcock et le rêve" in: *Hitchcock et l'art: coincidences Fatales*. Sous le direction de Dominique Païni and Guy Cogevai. Paris and Milano: Centre Pompidou and Mazzotta. pp. 41-50

Staiger, Janet (1989) "Securing the Fictional Narrative as a Tale of the Historical Real" in: *South Atlantic Quarterly* 88(2): 393-413

Stam, Robert (2000) "Beyond Fidelity: The Dialogics of Adaptation" in: *Film Adaptation*. Edited and with an introduction by James Naremore pp. 54-76. London: The Athlone Press

Starkie, Walter [n.d.] "Carmen and the tarots". From file on *Carmen* (1999). Paris: La Bibliothèque-Musée de l'Opéra National de France

Sterritt, David (1993) *The Films of Alfred Hitchcock*. New York and Cambridge: Cambridge University Press

Sullivan, Karen (1999) *The Investigation of Joan of Arc*. Minneapolis, MN & London: University of Minnesota Press

Tambling, Jeremy (1987) *Opera, Ideology and Film*. New York: St. Martin's Press

The Encyclopedia Americana (1961) The International Reference Work. vol. xvi 149-50. New York, Chicago, Washington D.C. Americana Corporation. First Published in 1829

Tibbetts, C. John (2004) "The Voice that Fills the House: Opera Fills the Screen" in: *Film & Literature Quarterly* (32)1: 2-10

Tisset-Lanhers (1870) *Procès de condamnation de Jeanne d'Arc*. Translated by Pierre Tisset & Yvonne Lanhers, 3 vols. Paris: Klincksieck

Trask, Willard (1996) (compiled and translated by) *Joan of Arc: In Her Own Words*. New York: Books & Co

Tynianov, Jury [(1981) 1927] "The Foundations of Cinema" in: *Russian Formalist Film Theory*. Ann Arbor: Michigan Slavic Publications

Usai, Paolo Cherchi (2001) *The Death of Cinema: History, Cultural Memory and the Digital Dark Age*. London: BFI Publishing

Van de Port, Mathijs (1998) *Gypsies, War and Other Instances of the Wild*. Amsterdam: University of Amsterdam Press

Venturi, Robert (1988 [1966]) *Complexity and Contradiction in Architecture*. Papers on Architecture. The Museum of Modern Art, New York, in association with Graham Foundation for Advanced Studies in the Fine Arts, Chicago

Verdi, Guiseppe (1845) *Giovanna d'Arco*. Lyric Drama in a prologue and Three Acts. Libretto by Temistocle Solera (performed in Italian) London Symphony Orchestra. Conducted by James Levine

Vervis, Constantine (1997) "Re-Viewing Remakes" in: *Film Criticism* vol. XXI/3

Warner, Marina (1979) *Joan of Arc: The Image of Female Heroism*. London: Weidenfeld and Nicholson

White, Hayden (1974) "The Historical Text as Literary Artifact" in: *Clio* (3): 277-303

— (1988) "Historiography and Historiophoty" in: *American Historical Review*, (93): 1193-1199

— (1996) "The Modernist Event" in: Vivian Sobchack (ed.) *The Persistence of History* pp.17-38. AFI Film Readers, New York and London: Routledge

Williams, Linda (2002) "When the Woman Looks" in: Mark Jancovich (ed.) *Horror, The Film Reader* pp. 61-66. London and New York: Routledge

Willemen, Paul (1975) "Notes Towards the Construction of Readings of Tourneur" in: P. Willemen & C. Johnston (eds.) *Jacques Tourneur*. Edinburgh

Wilson, Lambert (ed.) (1987) *Cinéma et Opéra: L'avant scene*. Dossier special, *Opéra* no. 98, *Cinéma* no. 360. Mai, 1987

Wittgenstein, Ludwig (1953) *Philosophical nvestigations*. New York: Macmillan

Wollen, Peter (1980) "Manet: Modernism and Avant-Garde" (A Response to Timothy Clark [1980] "Manet's *Olympia*") in: *Screen* 21(2): 15-25

Wood, Robin (1965) "Psycho" in: *Hitchcock's Films*. pp. 112-123. USA: AS Barns and Co Inc

Wyschogrod, Edith (1998) *An Ethics of Remembering: History, Heterology, and the Nameless Others*. Chicago and London: The University of Chicago Press

Yervasi, Carina (1999) "The Faces of Joan: Cinematic Representations of Joan of Arc" in: *Film & History* (29)3-4: 8-19

Young, Robert (1990) *White Mythologies: Writing History and the West*. London and New York: Routledge

Zanger, Anat (1986) *The Trailer as Mediator*. MA Thesis, Tel-Aviv University. Supervised by Menachem Brinker. Tel-Aviv University. Comparative Literature

— (1993) *Cinematic Versions- Originality as Repetition*. Ph.D. dissertation [English] supervised by Brian McHale. Tel-Aviv University, School for Cultural Studies

— (2001) "The Cinematic Remake: Repetition, Serialization and Spectacle" [English] in: *Assaph Kolnoa: Studies in Cinema & Television* in: *La longue durée - Framing in Series, Serial & Other Macaroni Forms*. Tel-Aviv University, Faculty of the Arts (2): 55-71

— (2001) "On the Writing of a Cultural Trauma" [Hebrew] in: *An Overcoat for Benjamin (Part II)* pp. 308-327. Ziva Ben-Porat (ed.) Literature, Meaning, Culture no. 28. Porter's Institute for Poetics and Semiotics, Tel-Aviv University-Hakibbutz Hameuchad

— (2003) "Desire Ltd: On Romanies, Women, and Other Smugglers in *Carmen*" published in *Framework-The Journal of Cinema and Media* vol. 44(2): 81-94, Fall, 2003. Special issue on Cinematic Images of Romanies. Guest editor: Dina Iordanova. New York

— (2004) "Joan of Arc Masked in Historical Realism" in: *History and Memory: A Dangerous Relationship*. Edited by Haim Bresheet, Shlomo Sand & Moshe Zimmermann pp. 273-292. The Zalman Shazar Center for Jewish History: Jerusalem

Žižek, Slavoj (1991) *Looking Awry: An Introduction to Jacques Lacan Through Popular Culture*. Cambridge, Mass. and London, England: The MIT Press

— (1993) "Eastern Europe's Republic of Gilead" in: Chantal Mouffe (ed.) *Dimensions of Radical Democracy: Pluralism, Citizenship, Community*. London

— (2001) "Is There a Proper Way to Remake a Hitchcock Film?" Unedited as it appears in Lacanian Ink at www.Lacan.com. Or in: *Enjoy Your Symptom Jacques Lacan in Hollywood and Out*. London and New York: Routledge (2nd edition) especially pp. 206-7.

Filmography

24 HOUR PSYCHO (1993) a video installation directed by Douglas Gordon

A BURLESQUE ON CARMEN (1916) directed by Charlie Chaplin with Edna Purviance as Carmen. Essanay, USA

ALIEN III (1992) directed by David Fincher with Sigourney Weaver as Ripley. 20th Century Fox and Brandywine Productions, USA

BREAKING THE WAVES (1996) directed by Lars von Trier with Emily Watson as Beth. Argus Film Produktie, Denmark/France

CARMEN (1915) directed by Cecil B. DeMille with Geraldine Farrar as Carmen. Lasky Feature Play Company, USA

CARMEN (1915) directed by Raoul Walsh with Theda Bara as Carmen. William Fox, USA

CARMEN/GYPSY BLOOD (1918) directed by Ernst Lubitsch with Pola Negri as Carmen. Projektions-Ag "Union", Germany

CARMEN (1926) directed by Jacques Feyder with Raquel Meler as Carmen. Film Albatros, Sequana Films, France

CARMEN (1931) directed by Cecil Lewis with Marguerite Namara as Carmen. British International Pictures, UK

CARMEN (1933) directed by Lotte Reiniger (Silhouette animated film). Lotte Reiniger Films, Germany

CARMEN (1936) directed by Anson Dyer (animated version) Angila Films.UK

CARMEN (1942-45) directed by Christian-Jaque with Viviane Romance as Carmen. Dis-cina, Invicta Film and Scalera Films S.p.a. France/Italy

CARMEN (1943) directed by Luis César Amadori with Niní Marshall as Carmen. Argentina Sono Film S.A.C.I., Argentina

CARMEN (1980) directed Dirk Sanders, choreographed by Roland Petit with Zizi Jeanmaire as Carmen. Studio Kultur and FR3 Telmondis, France

CARMEN (1983) directed by Carlos Saura with Laura del Sol as Carmen. Emiliano Piedra PC, Spain

CARMEN (1984) directed by Francesco Rosi with Julia Migenes-Johnson as Carmen. Société des Establissements Gaoument, Italy

CARMEN (1989) directed by Makoto Sato and Akira Sugiura, Japan

CARMEN (2003) directed by Vicente Aranda with Paz Vega as Carmen. Star Line TV Productions S.L., Spain

CARMEN: A HIP HOPERA (2001) directed by Robert Townsend with Beyoncé Knowles as Carmen Brown. MTV, USA

CARMEN JONES (1954) Otto Preminger with Dorothy Dandridge as Carmen
Jones. Carlyle Productions, Twentieth Century-Fox Film Coporation, USA

CARMEN VAN HET NOORDEN, EEN/CARMEN OF THE NORTH, A (1919) directed by
Maurits H. Binger and Hans Nesna with Annie Bos as Carmen. Hollandia,
the Netherlands

CASABLANCA (1942) directed by Michael Curtiz,Warner Bros, USA

CITIZEN KANE (1941) directed by Orson Welles. Mercury Productions Inc and
RKO Radio Inc, USA

DAS MÄDCHEN JOHANNA (1935) directed by Gustav Ucicky with Angela Sallo-
ker as Johanna. UFA, Germany

DIE BLONDE CARMEN/THE BLONDE CARMEN (1935) Victor Janson, with Martha
Eggerth as Carmen. Cine-Allianz Tonfilmproduktions GmbH, Germany

DRESSED TO KILL (1980) directed by Brian de Palma. Filmways Pictures, USA.
GIOVANNA D'ARCO (1990) Werner Herzog and Keith Cheetham with Susan
Dunn as Giovanna, NVC/ Teatro Comunale di Bologna, Italy/Germany

GIOVANNA D'ARCO AL ROGO [JOAN OF ARC AT THE STAKE] (1954) Roberto Rossellini with Ingrid Bergamn as Giovanna, Franco-London Films. France/Italy

HALLOWEEN (1974) directed by John Carpenter. Compass International Pictures
USA

JEANNE D'ARC (1900) directed by Georges Méliès with Louise d'Alcy. Star Films,
France

JEANNE D'ARC (1908) directed by Albert Capellani. Pathé, France

JEANNE LA PUCELLE (1993) directed by Jacques Rivette with Sandrine Bonnaire
as Jeanne. France 3 Cinéma and La Sept Cinéma, France

JOAN OF ARC (1948) directed by Victor Fleming with Ingrid Bergman as Joan.
Sierra Pictures and RKO, USA

JOAN OF ARC [THE MESSENGER] (1999) directed by Luc Besson with Milla Jovovich as Joan. Gaumont and Leeloo Productions, France

JOAN THE WOMAN (1916) directed by Cecil B. DeMille with Geraldine Farrar as
Joan. Paramount, USA

KARMEN GEÏ/CARMEN (2001) directed by Joseph Gaï Ramaka with Djeïnaba
Diop Gaï as Karmen. Zakrianka Productions et al., Senegal & France

KARUMEN KOKYO NI KAERU/ CARMEN COMES HOME (1951) directed by Keiske
Kinoshita with Hideko Takamine as Lily Carmen. Shochiku Films Ltd, Japan

LA CARMEN DE RONDA/CARMEN FROM GRANADE (1959) directed by Tulio De-
micheli with Sara Montieti. Producciones Benito Perojo S.A, Spain

LA MERVEILLEUSE VIE DE JEANNE D'ARC (1928) directed by Marc de Gastayne
with Simon Genevois as Jeanne. Aubert-Natan, France

LA PASSION DE JEANNE D'ARC (1927-28) directed by Carl Dreyer with Renée Falconetti as Jeanne. Stégle de Films, France

LA TRAGÉDIE DE CARMEN/CARMEN'S TRAGEDY (1984) directed by Peter Brook with Eva Saurova/Hélène Delavaout /Zehava Gal as Carmen. Bentwood Television Productions, Channel 4, Antenne 2 et al., UK & France

LOLA RENNT (RUN LOLA RUN) (1998) directed by Tom Tykwer. X-Filme Creative Pool, Germany

MOONSTRUCK (1987) directed by Norman Jewison. MGM, USA

NACHALO [LE DÉBUT] [THE GIRL FROM THE FACTORY] (1972) directed by Gleb Panfilov with Inna Tchourikova as Pasha/Joan Studio Len Films, USSR

PRÉNOM CARMEN/FIRST NAME: CARMEN (1983) directed by Jean-Luc Godard with Maruschka Detmers as Carmen. Sara Films, JLG Films and Films A2, France

PRETTY WOMAN (1990) directed by Garry Marshall. Silver Screen Partners and Touchstone Pictures, USA

PROCÈS DE JEANNE D'ARC (1962) directed by Robert Bresson with Florence Carres as Jeanne. Agnès Delahaie, France

PSYCHO (1960) directed by Alfred Hitchcock with Janet Leigh as Marion. Shamley Productions, USA

PSYCHO II (1983) directed by Richard Franklin. OAK and Universal Studio, USA

PSYCHO III (1986) directed by Anthony Perkins. Universal Studio, USA

PSYCHO IV: THE BEGINNING (1990) directed by Mick Garris. Smart Money Productions and Universal TV, USA

PSYCHO (1998) directed by Gus Van Sant with Anne Heche as Marion. Imagine Entertainment and Universal Studio, USA

SAINT JOAN (1957), directed by Otto Preminger with Jean Seberg as Joan. Wherel Productions, USA

TEXAS CHAINSAW MASSACRE (1974) directed by Tobe Hooper. Vortex, USA

THE LOVES OF CARMEN (1927) directed by Raoul Walsh with Dolores del Rio as Carmen. Fox Film Corporation, USA

THE LOVES OF CARMEN (1948) directed by Charles Vidor with Rita Hayworth as Carmen. The Backworth Corporation with Columbia Pictures Corporation, USA

THE MAN WHO KNEW TOO MUCH (1956) directed by Alfred Hitchcock, Filwite Production and Paramount Pictures, USA

VIVRE SA VIE (FILM EN DOUZE TABLEAUX) (1962) directed by Jean-Luc Godard. Les Films de la Pléiade and Pathé cinéma, France

WEST SIDE STORY (1961) directed by Jerome Robbins and Robert Wise. Beta Productions, Mirisch Films and Seven Arts Productions, UK

WHILE THE CITY SLEEPS (1956) directed by Fritz Lang. Thor Productions, USA

ZELIG (1983) directed by Woody Allen. Orion Pictures Corporation, USA

Credits

A Burlesque on Carmen (1916) directed by Charlie Chaplin, with Edna Purviance as Carmen. Essanay, USA. Picture from BFI archive courtesy of mr.Tom T. Moore, President of Reel Media International
ill. II b

Alien III (1992) directed by David Fincher, with Sigourney Weaver as Ripley. 20th Century Fox and Brandywine Productions, USA. Picture by ASAP
ill. VII b

Carmen (1915) directed by Cecil B. De Mille, with Geraldine Farrar as Carmen. Jesse L. Lasky Feature Play Company, USA. Private collection
ill. II a

Carmen (1983) directed by Carlos Saura, with Laura del Sol as Carmen. Emiliano Piedra PC, Spain. Picture from ASAP collection
ill. III a

Carmen (1984) directed by Francesco Rosi, with Julia Migenes-Johnson as Carmen. Société des Establissements Gaoument, Italy. Pictures by ASAP collections
ill. I and VIII b

Carmen: A Hip Hopera (2001) directed by Robert Townsend, with Beyoncé Knowles as Carmen Brown. MTV, USA. Private collection
ill. IV b-d

Carmen Jones (1954) directed by Otto Preminger, with Dorothy Dandridge as Carmen Jones. Carlyle Productions, Twentieth Century-Fox Film Coporation, USA. Picture from ASAP collections
ill. III b

Hofstadter, D.R. (1985a [1982]) "Variations on a Theme as the Crux of Creativity", in: *Metamagical Themes: Questing for Essence of Mind and Pattern*, p. 243. New York: Penguin
table 2, p. 105

Hofstadter, D.R. (1985b [1982]) 'Metafont, Metamathematics and Metaphysics: Comment on Donald Knuth's Article 'The Concept of Meta-Font'" in: *Metamagical Themes: Questing for Essence of Mind and Pattern*, p. 251. New York: Penguin table 1, p. 31

Joan of Arc (1948) directed by Victor Fleming, with Ingrid Bergman as Joan. Sierra Pictures and RKO, USA. Picture from ASAP collections
ill. VII a

Joan of Arc (*The Messenger*) (1999) directed by Luc Besson, with Milla Jovovich as Joan. Gaumont and Leeloo Productions, France. Picture from ASAP collections
ill. VIII a

Joan the Woman (1916) directed by Cecil B. De Mille, with Geraldine Farrar as Joan. Paramount, USA. Picture from BFI archives, courtesy of Mr. David Shepeard Film Preservation Association, INC, USA
ill. VI a

Olympia (1865) Edward Manet
ill. IV a

Psycho (1960) directed by Alfred Hitchcock, with Janet Leigh as Marion. Shamley Productions, USA. Picture from ASAP collections
ill. V a

Psycho (1998) directed by Gus Van Sant, with Anne Heche as Marion. Imagine Entertainment and Universal Studio, USA. Picture from ASAP collections
ill. V b

Saint Joan (1957) directed by Otto Preminger, with Jean Seberg as Joan. Wherel Productions, USA. Picture from ASAP collections
ill VI b

Index

Film Culture in Transition
General Editor: *Thomas Elsaesser*

Film Front Weimar: Representations of the First World War in German Films of the Weimar Period (1919-1933)
Bernadette Kester

Camera Obscura, Camera Lucida: Essays in Honor of Annette Michelson
Richard Allen and Malcolm Turvey (eds.)

Jean Desmet and the Early Dutch Film Trade
Ivo Blom

City of Darkness, City of Light: Émigré Filmmakers in Paris 1929-1939
Alastair Phillips

The Last Great American Picture Show: New Hollywood Cinema in the 1970s
Thomas Elsaesser, Alexander Horwath and Noel King (eds.)

Harun Farocki: Working on the Sight-Lines
Thomas Elsaesser (ed.)

Herr Lubitsch Goes to Hollywood: German and American Film after World War I
Kristin Thompson

Cinephilia: Movies, Love and Memory
Marijke de Valck and Malte Hagener (eds.)

European Cinema: Face to Face with Hollywood
Thomas Elsaesser

Hitchcock's Motifs
Michael Walker

The West in Early Cinema: After the Beginning
Nanna Verhoeff